Advance Praise for *A*

"I've fished against Mark in tournaments, shared hunting blinds with him, and have come to respect his unyielding courtesy and faith. Mark has lived a life of unique experiences, and I know readers will get to know and appreciate Mark as an old-school American individualist. Effective game management in the U.S. can be achieved by a consistent and knowledgeable harvest, carried out by ethical hunters like Mark Shepard."
Larry D. Martoglio, Wildlife Biologist and Forest Ranger

"If living the outdoors life has always baffled you, this book is the key to understanding its mysteries!"
Todd Kersey, founder and owner of BassOnline.com

"Mark Shepard is a true American outdoorsman that you would love to hang with anytime. Read his book and see for yourself. And I bet you'll learn something you didn't know, and maybe change your mind about something you did."
Tim O'Neil, Marketing Director, Wildlife Foundation of Florida

"The bottom line of Mark's message is to: Get out of the house. Have fun. Go fishing, hunting, boating, camping, hiking, meet people, and make friends. It's healthier for your body, mind, and soul rather than being confined to four walls, mesmerized with the cyber world of today's electronics."
Tom Martin, Chicago Police Officer (retired)

A Guiding Life

Living, Fishing and Hunting the American Dream

Mark Shepard
with Phil Fragasso

Erewhon Press

For my mom,
Sandy

Contents

Section Three: Coming Full Circle

Prologue

A Caribbean Cowboy

By the standards of most middle-income working Americans, I've led a rough life and have very little to show for it. I grew up dirt poor in a remote area of rural Florida. My parents split up when I was ten, and my brother and I were raised by my mother and grandmother. I attended high school for a grand total of two weeks, and I started working full time on a commercial fishing boat when I was fourteen.

Today, even after a reasonably successful career as a professional bass fisherman and guide, I wouldn't be able to feed my family without the meat I harvest from hunting and fishing. My wife and I moved out of our home because of damage from Hurricanes Charley and Wilma, and the insurance money we received was barely enough to repair the major structural damage let alone bring the house back to its original condition. We were forced to go back to renting until we could save enough to buy or build a home of our own.

Despite all that, I truly feel blessed. I have a wonderful wife and two sweet, intelligent daughters. I have a truck and a bass boat. (And I know exactly what you're thinking: "If your boat is worth more than your house, you're a redneck." It is.

And I am.) I live on the edge of Lake Okeechobee, one of the best – and most beautiful - bass fishing lakes in the world; and I spend most of my time outdoors enjoying the natural beauty of all that God has given us. Fortunately, that's how I've spent the vast majority of my life.

I was born in 1965 in Hamilton, Ohio. We lived in a small wood-frame house on my grandparents' twenty-seven acre tree farm. My grandparents' home was a unique design built into the side of a hill with two stories on one side and one on the other. We lived in the smaller house until I was five when my grandfather passed away. We then moved into the bigger house with my grandmother while my uncle moved into the smaller house with his wife. We were a tight-knit family that had a lot of fun together.

One of my oldest and fondest memories was sitting on my mom's lap, holding a simple cane pole, and fishing on the farm pond. I distinctly remember being hypnotized by the water and the magical experience of fishing. My dad wasn't much into fishing; but he made it a point to drive my brother, Chris, and I around so we could fish in all the local ponds. From the time we were little boys, my dad also taught us how to shoot; and he always stressed the importance of gun safety. In addition to my mom and dad, it was really my grandfather who got me hooked on the outdoor life. He especially loved fishing and inspired me to make a life of it. As a little boy I would go into grandpa's garage and stand there in awe looking at his collection of rods and reels. Sometimes Chris and I would open grandpa's tackle box and carefully examine each of the lures. We'd each pick out a lure and weave it through the air, imagining the way it might move in the water. Every lure with their varying textures, shapes and color combinations told a different story, and we longed for the day when we would know what lure to use in what situation. And we longed for our grandfather to teach us. I know he wished the same.

My grandfather's dream was to someday sell the family farm, move to Florida and open a fishing resort. He planned to get into the bait business and help service the booming tourist industry. Grandpa died in 1970 before he could make that dream come true, but my grandmother was determined to realize the vision she had shared with her husband. It took a few years to sell the farm, but when I was ten my grandmother purchased a fishing resort on South Hutchinson Island in Fort Pierce, Florida; and my mom, dad, brother and I moved down there with her to start a new and exciting life.

We had visited this part of Florida on vacation trips for as long as I could remember, and I'd always loved it. But actually getting to live on the island, with its tropical atmosphere and perfect weather - all surrounded by water and huge populations of every species of fresh and salt water fish you can think of - made me feel like I was in paradise.

But even paradise can have a down side. When my grandmother bought the resort, it pretty much wiped out our family savings and we were saddled with a sizable mortgage on the resort. My dad left shortly after we arrived in Florida and never came back. My brother and I were forced to grow up fast and take on a lot of responsibility. Along with my mom and grandmother, we learned to work together to get through the lean times, especially in the summer when the tourists disappeared.

There were many times when we didn't have enough money to buy groceries. We struggled a lot, but we struggled in private. Most people would see our real estate and assume we were wealthy – not realizing all the overhead expenses we had to carry.

While groceries were often hard to come by, fish were plentiful. My brother and I would grab a couple of nets, wade into the water, and scoop up shrimp, clams, oysters and small fish by the dozen. It's no exaggeration to say that we lived off the water. One end of our property dropped off straight down into the water and you could see clear through to the bottom. The water was about thirty-feet deep, with lots of ledges and reefs, and just loaded with lobsters. There were many times when we couldn't afford to have bacon or sausage for breakfast; but I'd get up early, throw on my mask and fins, dive around the rocks, and pull up two or three lobsters. Grandma would saute them in butter and we'd have lobster and eggs for breakfast. To this day, my favorite meal is fried fish and eggs. And if you add in some cheese grits, you'll see me eating with a grin the size of a largemouth lunker.

As hard as Chris and I worked to help out my mom and grandmother, we still had plenty of time for fun. Looking back, I'm so happy to have grown up in a rural setting in the decades of the 1970s and 80s. I'm sure I sound like an old man when I say this, but my generation was the last to grow up without all the electronic devices that kids have today. We didn't have video games, computers or cellphones. We did have a television, but we had to lift our butts off the couch to change the channel. We went to our friends' homes to talk and play and we organized fishing trips, baseball games and touch football games all on our own without our parents' help (or interference). Our parents pushed us outdoors to play, and we wanted to be outside. Many of today's kids just don't spend enough time outside enjoying the weather and nature. It's sad to me because I remember waking up every day as a kid and wondering what kind of adventure I would experience before I went back to bed that night.

For a couple of Ohio farm boys like Chris and me,

Florida was a whole different world. The kids we met thought we talked funny, and we thought their southern drawls sounded even funnier. Most of the friends we made in Florida were surfer kids and they called us Caribbean Cowboys. Despite their love of the ocean, surfing and diving, many of the kids seemed to take the natural beauty that surrounded them for granted. They were all good people, but they wanted to party every single night. And that partying lifestyle got some of them killed, snuffing out their potential before it had a chance to blossom.

One of the first victims was my seventeen-year-old former girlfriend. She was drinking while driving and, at age nineteen, I was a pallbearer at her funeral. Two years later I attended the funeral of my best friend, Ben – a great kid who I had done everything with: surfing, fishing, and diving. Hardcore partying became his primary interest and, one night after a particularly heavy binge, he totaled his car and we lost him. He was cremated and, with a bunch of mutual friends, we sprinkled his ashes from Dynamite Point into the Fort Pierce Inlet and went swimming with him for the last time.

My brother and I were not immune to this reckless behavior, and we'd get caught up with it once in a while. We'd go out with friends on a Friday night, and we'd usually have plans to go out fishing or diving early the next morning. We'd be ready to call it a night early, but our friends would urge us to have just one more. Well before we'd know it, morning had come around and we'd be suffering with splitting hangover headaches. We'd spend the day sick in bed – sick to our stomachs with the hangover and heartsick about losing a full day of outside adventures. The good news is that those few transgressions served as strong life lessons and reminded us why we didn't drink and party to excess. I love a cold beer on a hot day as much as the next guy, but I'm a total lightweight when it comes to drinking and can't deal with a hangover. The same goes for Chris.

When I look back on all my friends who never saw thirty years of age, I get chocked up and vow to continue preaching about how important it is for parents to get their kids involved with something. And it doesn't have to be fishing and hunting like it was for me. It could be something as simple as hiking, camping, or biking. It could be a sport like baseball, soccer or golf, or a school activity like debating or the arts. The key is to find something that interests their young minds and bodies. It will keep them active and fit and help them stay away from activities that are destructive to their lives, their families and their communities.

One of my very earliest memories is watching television and seeing images from the Vietnam War. I remember going out into the backyard, walking around my grandparents' farm, and feeling proud to be an American and lucky to live in such a beautiful and peaceful country.

Today I feel just as proud and lucky, and I do indeed feel blessed. My story is a simple one, and I share it with the hope that I can encourage Americans from all around the country – from Red states and Blue states, young and old, rich and poor – to embrace the values that our nation was founded upon. We're still the greatest country that the world has ever known but, like my deceased buddies who took too much for granted, we often lose sight of what's truly important and what truly matters. The rate of change in America and around the rest of the world is accelerating, and that makes an understanding of history and our individual and shared experiences especially critical.

It's been said that the past is prologue, and that's how I'd like you to view this book. It's my prologue, and hopefully it will contribute in some small way to your own future.

Section One:

The School of Life

MARK SHEPARD

Chapter 1

A Little Piece of Heaven

I had the good fortune to grow up in one of the most peaceful and beautiful places on earth. South Hutchinson Island is a barrier island on the eastern coast of central Florida about seventy miles north of Palm Beach. Living on an island has both advantages and disadvantages, but as a kid all I saw were the former. There's something about being on and near the water that soothes the soul. Water has a magical effect on everybody and opens up a world of opportunity for fun and adventure for kids of all ages.

We moved to the island when I was ten, after my grandfather died. I remember driving around with realtors and looking at real estate, and I was so excited when we purchased and moved into the fishing resort. Now, when I say "fishing resort," you're probably thinking about the kind of resort you'd find on one of the Caribbean islands, but it was nothing like that. Hutchinson Island was originally part of a military base; and when the military left, many of the officers' quarters and similar buildings were turned into fishing resorts. Ours was one of those resorts.

When we first arrived on the island we were all

together as a family. My mom, dad, and brother moved into the house, while my grandmother and I settled into an apartment in the hotel, while an addition to the house was being built. The "all of us together" image didn't last for long. My parents got divorced shortly after we arrived in Florida. Then, after construction was completed on the house and my grandmother and I moved in, my grandmother had a brain aneurism. It was really bad. Grandma didn't recognize any of us, and she started hallucinating, seeing snakes and stuff. It was absolutely horrible. We all took turns taking care of her. Feeding her and cleaning her. Chris and I had school and mom was trying to get the business going, so my mom realized that we had to put grandma into a nursing home. We really had no choice, but it felt like my world had collapsed. I'd lost my grandfather and left friends back in Ohio, then my parents split up, and now my grandmother didn't even know who I was. My grandmother had been the anchor of the family. She was a very Christian woman, who loved everyone and never said a bad word about anyone. She was my best friend and I was terrified of losing her.

Mom, Chris and I would visit grandma all the time, but it was always a sad occasion and at least one of us usually ended up crying. One Sunday we all went to church and then went to the nursing home to see grandma. When we walked into the home, grandma was down the hall. She saw us and started to shout out, "Sandy, Mark and Chris, oh my gosh, where have you been? Why am I here? What the heck is going on? I've been wondering where you've been. I've been worried sick about you."

It was one of the most mind-blowing things I've ever witnessed. All of a sudden grandma remembered everything. Her mind and all its faculties had come back. It was absolutely shocking, but we wasted no time. We packed up her stuff right then and there and brought her back home. We still had to take care of her and she had to have major brain surgery, but she came back 100% and lived to be almost 87 years old. Grandma died on September 8, 2001; and I believe that God took her away from this world so she wouldn't have to suffer through the horror of 9/11.

After my dad left and my grandmother got sick, the little savings we had disappeared fast and we were stone cold broke. I remember watching my mom staring at a pile of bills, holding her head in her hands and crying. She had no idea how we'd be able to keep the place, but she vowed to accomplish just that.

Our little fishing resort consisted of a house on one side of the property and seven efficiency apartments on the other side. Most of the people who stayed with us had been coming to the island for years. We had a group of farmers from West Virginia who'd spend a couple of months each winter with us. These repeat customers were our bread and butter and they became like family. They spent most of their time just fishing right off our dock or from the shore. In fact, back in those days, no one really needed to go out on a boat. There was fantastic fishing from most any spot on the island.

When Chris and I weren't in school, we'd catch bait and keep the bait buckets full for our customers. We enjoyed being around our customers, helping them with their fishing equipment and providing tips on where to go to catch such and such a fish. Most of what we knew about fishing we picked up from the locals because my dad, before he left us, really didn't know a thing about fishing and had even less interest in learning. Here's a perfect example. Just before my parents got divorced, my father drove into town to get some fishing equipment for the resort. Chris and I went with him to the tackle shop and even at our young ages we could see that he had no idea what to get. My dad told the clerk that he wanted "some good stuff, some big stuff that's going to last and help us catch some big saltwater fish." Well this guy sold my dad a set of yacht fishing rods. They're very short fiberglass poles built like a broomstick and are clearly not built for casting. To complete the ugly picture, the guy outfitted the rods with huge Penn bait-casting reels that each weighed a ton and filled them with 100-pound test line.

As we left the tackle shop, my dad handed us the equipment to carry and proudly said, "Here you go boys." Chris and I looked at each other and then at him and said, "Are we gonna get a boat to go with these rods?" My dad shrugged his shoulders and said he was hoping to, but in the interim it was left it to us to figure out how to use this super heavy duty fishing equipment. We began by just dropping the line off the docks. We tried to cast with them, but it was a nightmare. Everyone who saw us said it couldn't be done. "They're boat rods," they would say in a patronizing tone, as though they were sharing some critical information that had escaped us poor, ignorant children.

In an effort to get away from these well-meaning but annoying fellow fishermen, Chris and I would load up our yard wheelbarrow and push it about a half mile to some jetties that jutted out into the ocean. We went there pretty often and ended up meeting two older black guys named Willie and Slick. Willie was from Jamaica, and he and Slick fished with the same kind of bait-casting reels that we had. The difference is that they seemed to know what they were doing. Chris and I were burning the skin off our thumbs trying to cast these ridiculous boat rods and control the spool with our thumbs. We started putting duct tape across our thumbs to keep some semblance of a thumbprint, and we learned to put water on the spool to cool it off, but we still struggled and made very little progress. So we watched closely as Willie and Slick cast their lines halfway across the Fort Pierce inlet. We were just amazed, and we were determined to learn from these master bait-casters. And we did.

Willie and Slick became really good friends, and we'd hang out together on the jetties and help out each other. Slick in particular became a good family friend; and because he knew our family situation, he'd take us places, like up to Okeechobee to go crappie fishing, and look out for us. He was just a real nice guy. We all loved him to death and I'll never forget him. And because of Willie and Slick, there wasn't a fishing pole on the planet that Chris and I couldn't handle.

Of course, just because you can handle the rod, doesn't mean you can handle the fish on the other end of the line. Chris and I used to fish with each other's rods and reels all the time. This particular day, I was fishing with one of the boat poles with a giant Penn bait-casting reel. At this point I had learned to cast the thing and had started wearing a leather shoulder harness to help bear the weight of the rod and reel. The reel was loaded with over 600 yards of heavy-duty line. I should also point out that I was still just a kid and weighed about 140 pounds. Chris had been the last one to use the rod and he had tightened the drag all the way down. It didn't occur to me to test the drag, though that was a mistake I never made again.

I had gone down to the seawall and caught a jack crevalle fish. A small jack is excellent shark bait so I brought it up to the dock and put a hook in its back. I tossed the rig out as far as I could and sat myself down on a lawn chair talking to some of our customers. I had the reel set for free-spooling so the jack fish could swim around and entice a bite. That particular reel made a clicking sound as line was pulled off. It's a sound I've always found comforting. The clicking was slow as the jack fish swam, but all of a sudden it started screaming as the line was being pulled from the spool. Everyone on the dock gathered around saying stuff like, "Oh my gosh, son, you got a bite, you got a bite." They're all excited and I nodded like this happened to me all the time, but my insides were all aflutter. I knew this was a big one and I knew I'd probably need some help bringing it in, but I played it cool and calm. And then I flipped the switch on the reel to engage the drag and try and slow down the line. That's when all hell broke loose. Like I said, Chris must have had the drag turned down as tight as he could get it. So when the drag engaged it ripped me right out of the chair and slammed me against the dock railing. The thing kept pulling and I got dragged down the dock, scrapping across the boards. The rod was rubbing against the railing and, because I was attached to the rod with a leather harness, I was totally out of control. A bunch of the customers jumped up and grabbed hold of me. They acted just in the nick of time because I was about to be tossed over the railing and probably would have drowned because there was no way I could have gotten out of the shoulder straps.

Once the customers had me in their grasp, I loosened the drag; but it still took three of us to hold the rod steady. The line was screaming straight out into the ocean like I'd hooked on to the back of a Cadillac. As this whole thing is playing out, my mind started racing with all kinds of crazy thoughts. I knew we didn't have a lot of money and I worried that I'd lose the whole rod and reel set-up. I worried that the line, which was high-end, expensive Ande monofilament, would be stripped clean. And I worried that I'd lose the fish and never know what I was fighting. In retrospect, I guess two out of three ain't bad. I didn't lose the rod and reel. The line finally did snap, but I was able to retrieve most of it. And to this day I don't know if I snagged a submarine or one really,

really big shark. That night I was lying in bed and reminiscing about what had just happened. And I was just thinking, "Thank you, God," because if there hadn't been people around to help me, that could have been the end of young Mark Shepherd right there. Game over.

While I'll never forget the one that got away, I'll also always remember the big one I caught when I was just ten years old. I was fishing from that same seawall when the line went out straight. The fish was pulling hard and I figured I had a shark or some other huge beast. It took me a long time, but I finally landed a 47-inch, 28-pound snook. It's still the largest snook I've ever caught and it was featured in an article in the local paper – along with a picture of me. That was a pretty cool experience for a 10-year-old kid and helped to cement my love affair with fishing.

I spent a lot of time fishing from that seawall, and I often used to pretend I had my own fishing show on television. When Chris and I weren't fishing, we'd hang around with the local fishermen soaking up their knowledge. At age eleven, for example, I started to learn how to mend fishing nets. The local fishermen – especially the older guys – took advantage of our interest and had us help them clean and maintain a lot of their equipment. It was a good tradeoff for both parties. We got the opportunity to learn and they got free labor.

I was always curious as a kid, and pretty fearless. One time I was swimming off the jetties where we used to go to get lobster. There was a little snow-white sand flat – an area we called the jam because it was where the beach and jetty came together – and it was a good spot to spearfish for flounder. I was swimming in a little deeper water, maybe six or seven feet deep. Up ahead of me I spotted a gigantic black shadow. Rather than shying away, which would have been the smart thing to do, I swam right up to it and saw it was a manta ray that seemed to be ill. This thing was gigantic. It had a 20-foot wingspan and probably weighed more than 2,000 pounds. I started rubbing its back and it lifted up off the bottom trying to swim. Before I knew what was happening I was sitting on the back of a manta ray and it was taking me for a ride. Even before this encounter, I had always been fascinated with mantas. They used to come in the inlet and free jump. We'd be sitting in the backyard relaxing or fishing off the dock and all of a sudden you'd swear somebody dropped a pickup truck out of an airplane. These bats would jump out of the water and land on their bellies with a huge splash. Most of the time you didn't see them jump, but you always heard them land.

We heard and saw a lot of crazy stuff from our property. One morning I was sitting on the back porch with my mom when I saw a fin come up in the water. I pointed it out to my mother and said, "That's a pretty good sized shark." The fin went under and then came back up again. This time the fin was a good two feet out of the water. We had plenty of sharks in the waters off our property and, by this time, I'd caught some monsters; but this one seemed exceptional. The fin went down again and then came up about four feet out of the water. It repeated the sequence and came out of the water about six feet. My heart stopped. This was no ordinary shark. Fact is, it probably wasn't a shark at all. But I had no idea what it was. We had a short-wave radio at the house so my mom could talk to Chris and me when we were fishing offshore; and I got on the radio and shouted to see if there were any boats in the vicinity of the Fort Pierce Inlet. A friend of ours, Michael, responded and said he was in the turning basin. I told Mike that we'd seen a six-foot-tall dorsal fin sticking out of the water, and then a bunch of other boaters jumped into the conversation suggesting that I'd been doing some kind of crazy drugs because there was no way I'd seen any such thing. The chatter continued all day with most of it at my expense, but the chatter stopped cold the next day. Mike was working the inlet and he called us on the shortwave, shouting, "I got it! I got it! I'm heading towards Jaycee Park and I've got it!" I picked up the handset and asked him what it was. He said he didn't know but he had it in his net, had hooked a gaff to it, and was dragging it to the Jaycee Park cove. I told him we'd meet him there and we hopped into mom's car and raced to the cove. Mike was already pulling into the cove when we got there, but he couldn't get all the way in. The thing he was dragging was so big and so heavy that it got stuck on the bottom. The water was churned up and brown, so we still couldn't tell exactly what it was. The marine patrol showed up and told us it was a sunfish that weighed a couple of thousand pounds. Sunfish are extremely rare and normally live in very deep water, but this one was sick and had come into the shallows. It was an odd-looking creature that was almost all head. It looked like someone had cut a fish in half and tossed away the back end. Not quite sure why it was designed this way, but I sure was excited about seeing it upfront and personal.

In addition to fishing, I spent a lot of my youth free diving and snorkeling. I used to free dive down to 30 feet and loved the total freedom of it. This particular morning I was free diving near the reef where I'd encountered the manta ray. I was looking for lobster and I spotted one that had settled itself underneath a ledge. I couldn't quite reach him so I went up to the surface for air. I went back down, wedged my body halfway underneath this ledge, and grabbed the lobster. As I started to back out, I felt something hit my leg and it made me slam on the brakes. I turned around and this thing hit me in the face and knocked my mask off. I just about crapped my pants and sucked in a bunch of saltwater. It took me a few seconds to register what the thing was – a freakin' manatee! He was just sitting in the water checking to see what I was up to. I went to the surface, straightened my mask, and then went back down to see my new friend. I'd played with several manatee before, but this one was a real curious fellow. He let me pet him and when I went to the surface, he'd go up with me. I swam with him for a while and then grabbed hold of his tail and he took me for a ride along the reef. I just held on and he just kept paddling and paddling. He finally got tired of it and he swished his tail and washed me back about ten feet. I guess he wanted to show me how big and bad he really was. But he put up with me for a good while and I really think he was enjoying it just as much as I was.

Life on the island wasn't all fun and games, of course. I still had to go to school; and while I was never all that interested in book learning, my mom and grandmother had always taught me to be respectful and diligent so I held my own in the classroom. But all that changed when I entered junior high school.

The school I went to was in a pretty rough town. There was a lot of racial tension and violence. Fights were a daily occurrence, stabbings were common and riots were all-too-frequent. I personally got cut a couple of times and my agriculture teacher had his life ruined. He got stabbed in the eye with a pencil that went right through his brain to the back of his skull. It was a terrifying and vicious environment, and to this day I've never seen so much hate in people. I was only a couple of years removed from a farm in Ohio, and I didn't know these kinds of problems and issues even existed.

I remember one time in particular when the principal and I got cornered by a whole group of kids who started beating on us. We were fighting back trying to get away, but they outnumbered us something like twenty against two. It was right after school so my mom and grandmother arrived in the car to pick me up. (I had started off riding my bike to school but the tires kept getting slashed, so my mom would drive me there and back.) Mom saw us from the parking lot and she revved up the Caddy. She caromed over the curb, screeched across the sidewalk, and started driving right across the lawn towards us. My grandmother was sitting in the passenger seat and said, "Sandy, I don't think you're allowed to drive on the grass." My mom didn't hesitate for a second and said, "Well today I am." She had the gas pedal floored and was sliding sideways across the grass. The kids saw the car coming and didn't know what kind of a maniac was behind the wheel, so they all took off running. The police showed up a while later, but they'd seen this kind of thing a thousand times before and nothing ever came of it.

I wasn't allowed to go to normal classes in seventh and eighth grade. They put me in an "alternate school work program." Essentially they put all the biggest kids in this class and they made us mow grass and wash dishes.

It was the same kind of situation when I went to high school. They told me I had to be on a work program, so I was only going to class for a couple of hours. Then they loaded me up on a small bus and dropped me off at a job site. I hated it and told my mom that I was just going to have them bring me to the hotel and I would put that down as my job. Momma agreed and that went on for a week or so. I finally said to my mom that I wasn't getting anything out of school the way it was structured, and it would be better for me to get a real job and help out with all the bills. I don't think she was totally happy with my decision, but she understood.

Chris had also dropped out of high school after freshman year and went into commercial fishing. This happened to a lot of us who didn't get a fair shot. I don't know what it's like to go to a high school prom. I don't know what it's like to be a varsity athlete. I could've played high school football and probably would've been pretty damn good at it, but I never had the opportunity.

One of the things that I saw and learned as a kid was that the harder I worked, the more money I could make, the bigger boats I could own, and the more nets I could buy. Chris and I figured that out at a young age. When we were little kids back on the farm, everybody worked hard and worked together and I saw that if you wanted something in life you had to work for it. Out on the island, I saw a strong work ethic everywhere I looked. If you didn't work at the nuclear plant or in the commercial fishing industry, then you crossed the bridge every morning and worked on the mainland.

Unfortunately, a lot of our friends that lived in town had no drive whatsoever. They just sat around the house. And that kind of inactivity often turns into mischief. It turns into drug dealing and partying and carrying on. Many of my friends from those days ended up in prison and a bunch of them died violent deaths or overdosed. I could see where they were headed and it used to just break my heart. Chris and I always tried to get our friends involved in the activities we loved. We'd take them out fishing and hiking in the woods. That was our love, our passion. And I believe that if it wasn't for our love of the outdoors, there's no telling where we would have ended up.

Mother Nature saved our lives and I will always love her for that.

Chapter 2

Shark Week Every Week

The movie *Jaws* came out in 1975 when I was ten. My parents took me to see it in Ohio just before we moved to Florida. You can imagine the impression the movie made on me when I first started swimming, snorkeling and fishing in the waters around our new home. I can't say I was terrified; but I was certainly on high alert, and that image of the great white leaping out of the water was always in the back of my mind.

What's ironic about that memory is that shark attacks were far less common back then than they are today. The reason is that commercial fishing for sharks in Florida has been dramatically reduced due to a bunch of Federal regulations introduced in the mid-1990s. The upshot of those regulations is that the shark population is growing – and more sharks mean more close encounters with humans.

My first close encounter with a shark happened when I was about 12 years old. We had started attending services at Saint Andrews Church in Fort Pierce and I had gotten involved in one of the church's youth groups. I became buddies with the pastor's son, and one day we were swimming together at a youth group beach outing. We decided to go out to the closest reef and do a little snorkeling. The water was kind of choppy that day and visibility wasn't very good, but we headed out to the reef anyway. At one point we came up to the surface and treaded water as we talked. All of a sudden something hit me hard in the back right between my shoulder blades. The only thing I remembered was seeing a little white light and then I was gone. I woke up on a picnic table, coughing up salt water, with a crowd of people jammed in around me. My back felt like I'd been run over by a steamroller and I asked what had happened. The pastor's son, who was white as new fallen snow and trembling from head to toe, told me we'd been talking when I got pushed three or four feet through the water. He said a shark had come right over the top of my head and then started to swim towards him. He said he was frozen in place but the shark suddenly curved off, swam within two feet of him, and then took off. That boy – who was the same age as me and who I'm ashamed to say I can't remember the name of – literally saved my life. Everyone figured that the shark had been chasing a baitfish and had hit me running at full speed – probably swimming 30 miles an hour. The good news is that he squared off and hit me with his nose and didn't cut me with his teeth. I was plenty sore for a few days, but like all twelve-year-olds I healed up fast and was back in the water in no time.

Two years later I again came face to face with the ocean's fiercest creatures. I was with my mom and another family and we were diving off of Jensen Beach. The other family had a son about the same age as me, Todd, and we used to go free diving and spear fishing together. We were in water about 25- to 30-feet deep. I was very comfortable at that depth. I was pretty much part fish at that age, and so was Todd. We swam about 75 yards away from the boat and started diving near a reef. Todd was shooting spadefish; but because we already had quite a few in the cooler, I was taking my time. I was hoping to get a grouper and had passed over a couple of smaller fish looking for a decent size one. I came to the surface and Todd had just finished pulling off a spadefish and putting it in his goodie bag. He was trying to get his gun reloaded and we were both bobbing up and down with our heads out of the water. I saw a flash of a blacktip shark out of the corner of my eye and told Todd to dump the bag. I told him I had just seen a shark and he said, "Really?" I shouted back "Really!" He slid over closer to me and dropped the whole bag of spadefish into the water. I looked down in the water and saw that we were surrounded by sharks. They were everywhere. There must have been 40 or 50 of them – a whole school of blacktips and every one of them was a good seven to eight feet long. These were serious man-eaters. I felt something push up against my back and I saw a nose and an eyeball. The shark rolled up on my back and swooshed. When he swooshed, he gave me a road rash on my armpit and pushed me away in the water. Todd and I were trying to get back to the boat. My mom saw the sharks and was shouting at us to hurry. Todd's mom – who thought of herself as a high society woman but who reminded me of the kind of New Jersey housewife who would today be featured in the "Real Housewives" series – was shaking her head and saying no, those are just dolphins. My mom corrected her by saying that dolphins don't swim like that. All the while Todd and I were swimming like crazy trying to get back to the boat safely. Well blacktips are also known as spinner sharks and they do some crazy stuff in the water. If they want to hit something on the surface, they swim way down underneath the target and start spinning around and acting real goofy. Then they'll come straight up to the surface like a rocket and hit their prey at 40 miles an hour. So I saw one of them swim below me and start its pre-launch routine. I knew from experience in watching sharks that the only way to save myself was to dive down towards the shark. When blacktips see their prey do that they'll level out and abort their launch. And that's exactly what happened. I swam down five or six feet and the shark leveled out like a fighter jet and cruised on out. I came back to the surface and Todd and I kept swimming to the boat. When we finally got there Todd's dad helped him into the boat. I was still sitting in the water. I was wearing U.S. Divers Rocket fins but the little ladder on the back of the boat was barely wide enough for your foot. My mom was yelling at Todd's dad to help me. I was holding onto the ladder and saw another shark right underneath me. This one was a lot bigger than the other one and he started doing his wind-me-up, spinner-shark freak show. I wished that Star Trek's Scottie was there to "beam me up," but I took the situation into my own hands and lifted myself onto the outboard to get really tight to the boat in case he launched. Todd and his dad finally got me back onto the boat, and Todd's mom's was sitting there saying stuff like, "You guys are just trying to scare me. There's no shark out there. This is ridiculous. I'm trying to have a good time and you guys are acting like fools." My mom got mad as hell and she didn't get mad very often. She's a pretty sweet lady, but she also doesn't suffer fools. So my mom stood up and said, "You don't think there're sharks out there?" She picked up a handful of the spadefish we were using as bait and tossed them about five feet off the back of the boat. She told Todd's mom to watch what happens. It wasn't more than a couple of seconds before this eight-foot blacktip flew completely out of the water with the baitfish in its mouth. It was spinning like a top and its tail was a good four or five feet out of the water, which meant we had another eight feet of shark right above our heads. The shark hit its vertical peak and then came plummeting down. It just missed the boat, but it hit the water broadside and triggered a giant wave that crashed over the boat. Todd's mom was wearing a straw hat and the impact of the wave caused it to wrap right around her head. It was a hilarious sight and I started laughing, but she started freaking out and crying, so my mom hushed me. Everyone decided to call it a day and we headed back to dock.

Whenever I think about these experiences I realize it's an absolute miracle that I'm still in one piece and alive today. Especially because I've witnessed several episodes that didn't turn out so well.

One of my childhood friends, Whitey, was cast-net fishing with a bunch of us in the Indian River. We were all waiting to spot some fish so we could toss our cast nets when something started to swirl around Whitey. He wasn't in very deep – just a little above his waist. Well the water just blew real close to him, and he got jerked down. We saw a lot of splashing and turbulence in the water and then Whitey popped back up and dropped his net. He leaned over and grabbed hold of a shark – a shark that still had its teeth clenched onto his foot. Whitey was able to drag the shark over to where we could all help him and get the shark to release his foot. We then tied a rope around the shark's tail and hung it off a branch of an Australian pine tree. The shark hung there for at least five years and dried up in the sun like a piece of beef jerky. Whitey fared somewhat better. The shark had pulled the skin right off his foot and it was hanging off his toes like a wet sock. It was a nasty injury, made worse because the tussle in the water had driven sand deep into the wound. Obviously his foot never looked the same and he always walked with a limp, but that was okay with Whitey when he considered the alternative.

My most horrific experience with a shark attack happened right off our back yard in South Hutchinson Island.

My brother and I had just finished diving and were changing out of our diving gear. There was a bit of a storm rolling in, the tide was starting to change, and it was getting dark. There was another guy in the water diving with a friend. We saw him come up to the surface, roll over, and then get pulled back down. People started screaming, and Chris and I got back in our gear and jumped into the water. We swam all over the place looking for the guy. The current was getting really bad and we knew the odds were against finding him. After a while, the Coast Guard arrived and we got out of the water. They had helicopters and they were shooting off flares trying to light up the Fort Pierce Inlet. They searched all night long but they never found him. About five days later there were some divers out offshore from our house and they found the poor guy. My mom and I were there when they pulled him out of the water, and it was an ugly scene. His stomach was gone and there were catfish up in his chest cavity. It was a sad thing to see and it reminded us that diving anywhere at any time is dangerous.

But let me end on a more positive note. When I was a teenager, my friend, Ben, and I were going over to Dynamite Point to see a couple of girls we knew. Instead of taking one of the boats, we had the bright idea to swim across the Fort Pierce Inlet on a surfboard. We only had one surfboard but we figured we'd just kind of hold onto it and swim across. I mean how hard could it be? So Ben was on one side of the surfboard and I was on the other. We were swimming and paddling our way across the inlet like a couple of happy idiots when a shark came up underneath us. The water was boiling all around us and then we were lifted right up out of the water. The shark was looking at us with huge bug eyes, and we saw that the thing was gigantic. Ben and I came to the same conclusion at the same time and we scrambled to hop up onto the surfboard. Ben got up on it first, and then I got up and climbed onto his back to keep my feet out of the water. I'm sure we looked like a couple of gay guys trying to do some kinky things on a surfboard, but we were just terrified – screaming and paddling. After a while we saw the girls we were going to meet, Kristy and Kerry, in their boat and we start shouting and waving at them to come over. They're like, "Hey, guys. Whatcha doin?" And we're half delighted and half terrified to see them because we had to slip off the surfboard in order to grab onto and get into the boat. The prospect of dropping our legs and bodies into that water with the shark somewhere in the vicinity seemed like a lose-lose scenario. But we did it – making the transition from surfboard to boat as fast as humanly possible. It was another one of those close calls that I will never forget, and one that reminds me every day that the ocean is probably the most violent place on earth. It's a top-to-bottom food chain where everything is trying to kill everything else. And people need to remember that they become one of those "everythings" every time they enter the water.

Chapter 3

Mother Nature's A Bear

The way I figure it, the more time you spend outdoors, the more opportunity Mother Nature has to have a little fun and see how tough you really are. Well I've spent most of my waking hours outdoors, and Mother Nature has made the most of her opportunities to test my mettle.

My brother Chris and I used to do a lot of bass fishing with our buddy, Craig. Lake Okeechobee was our favorite fishing playground, but we were always exploring new lakes and ponds. We especially liked the Three Lakes Management Area in central Florida, partly because the fishing was great and partly because it was so isolated that we almost felt like explorers in an undiscovered land. There was one small lake out in the middle of nowhere that particularly caught our eye. Its bank was covered in saw grass all the way around; and the saw grass was real thick, sometimes extending as much as fifty yards from dry land into the lake. We figured it had to be a great fishing spot because it wasn't fished much. So we kept exploring and one day we found a spot where we could launch our Jon boat. It was a long trail through the saw grass, just wide enough for the Jon boat and just deep enough for a trolling motor. So we squeezed our way down the trail and into the open lake. And, man oh man, were we ever excited. We were having the time of our lives, catching bass, and trolling around this beautiful lake with no one else around for miles.

Fact of the matter is, we were having too much fun and weren't paying attention to what was going on around us. The weather started turning bad. It was like flipping a switch. All of a sudden it got overcast and dark, and then the rain started to pour down on us. We quickly realized that we had to head back to the truck, and just as quickly realized that the edges of the lake all looked pretty much the same. We circled and circled the lake but couldn't find the trail where we'd entered. In what seemed like a matter of minutes, it was pitch black – except for the occasional bolt of lightning – and we were drenched. We had no flashlights, no rain gear, and there was no one around to help us for miles and miles. We had nothing, and we were really spooked and unsure what to do. And by the way, this was mosquito heaven with those awful creatures swarming all around us. It was just about the worst place and worst situation to be lost.

We kept slowly trolling along the edge of the lake, trying to peek through the saw grass, and we finally found a little pocket that we thought was the boat trail. We motored the boat in and quickly hit a dead end. The rain was picking up and the Jon boat was filling up with water. Things were not looking good and we had to make a decision. We talked it over and decided to push the Jon boat through the saw grass until we found dry land. In retrospect, it was probably the only thing we could have done, but it was a very dangerous course of action. We were surrounded by gators, cottonmouth snakes, and poisonous spiders; and there were a lot of ways to get hurt or killed. The flipside is that the Jon boat could have sunk and we'd be in even worse trouble.

Craig and I jumped out of the boat and started dragging it through the saw grass. Every other step we'd either sink in the mud or step up onto something solid like a rock or tree stump. It was one of the scariest and most eerie things I've ever had to do. We were truly afraid for our lives. The only thing we could do was try and make as much noise as possible and hope we scared any critters away from us.

We pushed and pulled, and it seemed like the nightmare was never going to end. We were submerged all the way up to our shoulders in some places, and up to our waist most everywhere else. Finally the saw grass started thinning out a little bit, the water got shallower, and then we hit dry land. The three of us pulled the Jon boat up onto land, but there wasn't much celebrating because we still didn't have a clue as to where we were or how we'd get back to the truck. As crazy as it was to tromp through the water like we'd done, it would have been pure insanity to try to find the truck in pitch darkness. So we found ourselves a couple of big sticks and wrung out our tee-shirts as best we could. We ripped pieces of cloth from the tee-shirts, tied them to the sticks, and doused them with gasoline. Luckily my brother had a cigarette lighter that he'd kept in a waterproof plastic bag with his pack of Marlboros. Chris lit the makeshift torch and we all jumped backward as we saw a sea of faces looking at us. It was a herd of big black cattle. I'm not sure what they were doing there, but I guess if you're going to stumble upon a half-ton animal, we could have done a whole lot worse.

Despite the fact that we were now on dry land, we were still knee-deep in cow dung (both literally and figuratively). We needed to complete the mission by locating the truck, loading up the Jon boat and getting home to bed. We decided that Chris and Craig would follow the edge of the lake in search of the truck, and I would stay with the boat. So I watched them head off and watched the torch fade away in the distance. They told me later that the tee-shirt torches burned out fast, and they had to walk most of the way in darkness. They came upon a fence, climbed over it and walked right into the truck. It was pure dumb luck.

We were fortunate to have a lot of dumb luck that day. While Chris and Craig were looking for the truck, I was sitting in this boat waiting for them to return. I heard something slithering around in the back of the boat. I flicked my cigarette lighter to throw some light and I saw that a gator was trying to stick its snout over the boat to get to the fish we had kept on a stringer. At first I figured the worst was about to happen, but then I saw that the gator wasn't very big. I grabbed the wooden paddle that we kept in case the motor died and swung it like a baseball bat. I whacked the gator on the head and he took off and didn't return.

Chris and Craig finally arrived in the truck and we loaded up everything by the light of the headlights. At this point it was about three o'clock in the morning and we lived a couple of hours away. When we got home, my mom looked at us and didn't know whether to laugh or cry. We'd all been eaten up by the mosquitoes and were covered with welts. Our skin and clothes were coated with black soot from the water, and we smelled like swamp rats. After I showered and crawled into my nice warm, dry bed, I said an extra prayer for getting us home safe and sound.

I think the good Lord must have heard that prayer of thanks, because He chose to keep me safe on several other occasions. One day when I was living on South Hutchinson Island, my friend, Sam, asked me to help him set and field-test a small mackerel net and see what we could come up with. Sam had a 24-foot Suncoast with the wheelhouse at the front of the boat. The boat had a very small cabin where you could maybe lay down in a fetal position, but that's about all you could do. It was mainly used for storage. The weather wasn't looking too good that particular day, but Sam tempted me with an unplanned and sorely needed paycheck.

We headed out into the Atlantic but stayed within sight of land. The weather was changing rapidly from bad to horrible. But we were determined and we started setting the net. As we were running the net out, I happened to look up towards the front of the boat and saw a waterspout, which is basically a tornado on water. I couldn't really tell what direction it was going but I knew it wasn't very far from us. I called out to Sam, and when he saw the waterspout he started to panic. We both realized it would be impossible to get the net back onboard in time to avoid the waterspout, so we dumped the rest of it overboard and ran out the string. By this time the waterspout had gotten a lot closer, and rain started pouring down on us. It got so dark we couldn't see 15 feet in front of us. Sam was trying to steer the boat, but the waterspout had a mind of its own and started spinning the boat around. Now we couldn't tell which direction to head in even if we could take control of the boat. The waterspout was slinging the boat around like a cork, and we were scared to death. We crawled to the little cubby cabin and hunkered down, grabbing life jackets and hanging on to the built-in structure with all the might our terrified bodies could muster.

Just about the time we thought Christmas and birthdays would be permanently canceled, the rain and wind slowed. We waited a few minutes to make sure that Mother Nature wasn't giving us a head fake and peeked out of the cabin. The good news was that the boat was undamaged; the bad news was that we had no idea where we were or where the net was. The sea was still covered in a heavy fog, but Sam pointed the boat to where we thought landfall would be. We finally saw a bit of land and were able to get our bearings, but we still had no idea where the net was. Sam zig-zagged the boat in the general area of where we had started out and we looked for the net's buoys. We rode around for a couple of hours until we spotted one of the buoys in the distance. As we pulled up alongside it, I saw that the net had balled up into the biggest, most tangled-up mess you could ever imagine. Essentially we had a 500-yard long monofilament net that had been twisted, spun, and knotted into a solid clump that was bigger than the boat. We worked the rest of the day to get the net untangled and back into the boat, laid out the way it's supposed to be. The waterspout had ripped a lot of holes in the net and many hours of repair work were going to be required to make it usable again. So all-in-all it was a terrible day: we busted our butts until we couldn't move any more; we never caught a fish; we didn't make a nickel; and we had the snot scared out of us. Chalk up one for Mother Nature.

Chapter 4

My Deadliest Catch

I know that police officers and firefighters face the threat of death every single day but, in my humble opinion, commercial fishermen truly have the most dangerous jobs in the world. When you're boarding a boat that's headed out to sea, it's a moment that strikes at your soul. In your heart of hearts you know that when you say your good-byes to your loved ones, it might very well be the last time you see them.

Where I grew up on South Hutchinson Island, there were a lot of people and families involved in the commercial fishing industry. So I was exposed to the lifestyle at a very early age, and it was something I always assumed would become my life's work. My brother, being older, got a head start on me. He started working with a hook-and-line kingfish fisherman, and he was going out on the ocean when he was only 13 or 14 years old. I started out at around the same age working with one of my mom's friends as a spider pole fisherman. Spider pole fishing really reduces the sport to its most basic elements. You use a cane pole tied to a leader and a hook – with a piece of shrimp or other natural bait on the hook. There's no reel, fish finders or fancy technique.

When you hook a fish – usually a sea trout – you flip it up and onto the boat. Then you re-bait the hook and do it again. The "spider pole" name comes from the fact that you typically have six or eight poles splayed around the boat to increase the efficiency of what has to be the most inefficient of commercial fishing techniques.

As a kid, my bedroom was on the second floor facing out towards the water. Every day my brother and I watched the fleets of boats go in and out. There were a lot of one- and two-man commercial fishing operations based in Fort Pierce. They usually fished from small to mid-sized boats, usually 35 to 40 feet long, with a small cabin in the front and a flat top going all the way to the back of the boat. They'd mostly hand jig the lines and then use electric reels to pull in the fish. There were shrimp trawlers and scallop boats; but of all the fleets going out, the ones that impressed us the most were the roller rigs. These were bigger boats – most of them close to 60 feet long. That's where the serious money was and that's where I spent the bulk of my fishing career. It's also where I came face to face with the Lord and the Grim Reaper many times over.

As I described earlier, my school situation was terrible and it seemed much better for me to just go out and work. And the kind of work I wanted to do was focused solely on fishing. A friend of mine had a small inboard with a six-cylinder engine and I went into business with him. He and I had a lot of fun together. Sometimes for lunch we'd catch oysters, steam them on the manifold, and sprinkle them with Tabasco. We both had a passion for the commercial fishing business but we were very young and still had a lot to learn.

I recall one time when we were setting a pompano net just outside of the breakers down by the firehouse. With a pompano net, you place the tail end of the net and run it north or south, parallel to the coast, and then cup it to catch pompano. This particular time we were bringing the net in and all of a sudden it started pulling like crazy. We couldn't figure out what the heck was going on, but the next thing we know the net got pulled under the boat. The net got all tangled up in the props, and we were still trying to figure out what had happened when we saw it. It was the biggest nurse shark I'd ever seen. Nurse sharks aren't real aggressive about biting people, though they do have extremely powerful teeth and jaws. They eat conch shells and they break them like they were delicate light bulbs. They're pure muscle. Well this nurse shark was all wrapped up in the net and the net was wrapped up in the props. We quickly realized there was only one thing to do, so we jumped overboard and started cutting the net to free the shark. The water was pretty rough with four- and five-foot waves, so we had to hold onto the boat with one hand while cutting with the other. To add to the commotion, the shark was acting just like you'd expect a wild animal that had just been caught in a net to act – he was beating us to death trying to get free. Finally we got enough webbing cut that the shark could get out. He was happy, but we were still in the water trying to get the net untangled. One of our friends was running his boat close to the beach, and he saw our boat but couldn't see us in the water. He kind of panicked, thinking something terrible had happened, and came inside the breakers. Once he got there he couldn't get back out and ended up dry-docking his boat. So now we had two boats in trouble in the same spot at the same time. When we finally got our net mess straightened out and our boat running again, we tossed our friend a line and pulled his boat back out beyond the breakers. It's a fun story to tell now but it wasn't much fun at the time.

Another story that's also more fun to tell than it was to

experience occurred very early in my commercial fishing career. I was about 14 years old and I was working alongside Chris on a big boat called the Blue Jillian. At that point in my career I was a "striker," meaning I was purely a manual laborer whose job it was to set and strike the nets. It was exhausting and dangerous work but, like they say, "someone has to do it." The Blue Jillian was part of a fleet of about a hundred boats. The captain of the Galilean, one of the other boats in the fleet, radioed that they were in a serious situation and needed some major assistance. The Galilean was "rocked down," which meant the net was tangled in the reef, and they had a solid jag of fish. (Jags are big patches of net that are packed tight with fish.) The Galilean captain said they were taking on water and were going to lose their gear and all the catch. It turned into a panic on the Jillian as we rushed to help our fleet mate. Of course, getting there was the easy part. We were in eight-foot seas and we were trying to figure out how to get these two gigantic boats close enough together so a bunch of us could jump from the Blue Jillian to the Galilean. The captains of the two boats kept easing up to each other until they got as close as possible. The next step was for one of us to make the first jump. It was a scary moment. The sea was rising and falling with eight-foot swells, and one moment we were looking at the water line of the Galilean and then the next moment we're looking over the top of the wheelhouse. Essentially, one boat was going up while the other one was going down. There was no margin of error. Your jump had to be timed perfectly or you'd end up crushed and/or killed. The first striker made the jump safely with a picture-perfect landing. I was next. Because of my martial arts training, I was very agile and had excellent balance; but I'd never attempted anything like this and I'm not ashamed to say that my butt was tightly puckered. Chris was just as scared as I was and he was holding on to my arm with a death grip. He kept telling me to "Time it right, Mark. Time it right." When I jumped, the Blue Jillian was coming up and the Galilean was going down. I remember flying through the air and watching the Galilean's deck drop away from me. It was a surreal experience as I seemed to keep falling and falling. When I finally landed on the deck, I was thankful just to be alive. One more striker followed, and then the Blue Jillian backed off and we went to work.

The Galilean was a double-roller rigger. It was extremely powerful and a lot bigger than the Blue Jillian, almost 70 feet long. I'd never been on this boat before, but I knew what the other strikers and I had to do. The basic idea was to climb up the net like a ladder, and then have as many as eight guys start pulling down with all their body weight to get the roller to grab some fresh leads. It took a while, but we finally got it to bite the net; and this huge wad of fish starting coming onto the boat. And I mean a huge wad of fish. It was coming over by the thousands of pounds and we were directly underneath it, so we had thousands of pounds of fish coming over the top of our heads and covering us in fish slime like a glazed donut. We were still a little giddy about getting the roller moving again when the net gave way and knocked us all to the deck. We were slipping and sliding, and I fell through a hole into the holding tank where they kept their ice. I dropped down about eight feet to the bottom of the boat and landed in four feet of water and ice. To this day I don't know how the hell I got out of that hole, but I was out in a flash. I jumped up, grabbed the edge of the hole and did a pull-up to end all pull-ups with my boots and oilers full of water and ice. I was freezing my butt off, but I didn't have time to complain or worry about myself. I teamed up with the rest of the crew to get the net back on the roller and get all the fish onboard.

The last step was to shovel ice on top of the fish and then we booked it for home. And I chalked up one more near-death experience. They say what doesn't kill you only makes you stronger. If that were true, at this point in my life I probably could have gone toe-to-toe with the super hero of your choice.

The fickle seas, stormy weather, and equipment problems weren't the only dangerous aspects of commercial fishing. We also had pirates to deal with. Up until a few years ago that statement would have surprised most people. But with all the publicity about the pirate ships off the coast of Somalia, and the amazing and courageous rescue of an American sea captain by Navy SEALs back in 2009, the danger of pirates has come back into our national consciousness. For commercial fishermen, of course, that danger never left and was always front and center on our minds. That's why the crews I worked with – just like the crews on television's *Deadliest Catch* – always carried a fair amount of guns on board. We typically had an arsenal of assault rifles like M16 Bushmasters, along with an assortment of shotguns and hunting rifles. We'd frequently hear gunshots off in the distance and customs agents would often come by to check on us. They had the right to board the boat if they wanted, but it was pretty clear that we were just simple fishing folks so they usually just talked with us for a while and then headed into the night.

The closest encounter I had with pirates occurred one night when we were way out in the ocean fishing for kings. Pirates had their operation down to a science. They didn't bother boats that were moving, but rather focused on boats that had anchored down for the night. They would attack in the middle of the night when everyone except the watchman would be asleep. Their intent was not to rob – other than the weapons cache which was very desirable – but instead to use the boat for a couple of smuggling runs and then sink it or burn it. This particular night we were drifting for kingfish with a net that was almost two miles long. We had to tie the boat off at the windy end of the net to keep it tight and straight.

I was asleep downstairs with the other two crewmen. Chris was on watch duty when he saw a speeding boat on the radar. Anytime you're out there and you see a boat on radar going forty or fifty miles an hour, you know it's not a fishing boat so it's something to keep an eye on. The boat made a half-moon around us but stayed about a mile away. Then the boat started to move closer and Chris knew this was trouble and could get ugly very quickly. He stomped on the deck of the boat to wake us up and we knew immediately that something serious was going on. We poked our heads up and Chris yelled at us to "Get the guns, get the guns." In a situation like that we had no choice but to fight. We couldn't go anywhere dragging that huge net behind us; and even if we did release the net, the Blue Jillian was not built for speed and the pirates would have been on us in a nanosecond. So we positioned ourselves behind the gunnels and waited. We could hear the boat running and making half-moons around us. They had radar of their own and could tell that we were pulling gear, and they made sure to stay away from the net because they'd get all caught up if they tried to motor over it. Like most pirates, these guys knew what they were doing and would much prefer to sneak up on someone, steal the boat and get out of Dodge rather than get caught in a gunfight. Well this boat kept doing its half-moon route and then slowed down and started inching towards us. It was a black cigarette boat – or what the locals called a "go-fast boat." Black was the preferred color of pirates because it was almost impossible to see at night. This boat had no running lights which was strictly illegal, not to mention extremely dangerous. So at this point we knew this was the real deal. These were criminals with evil things on their mind. There's no denying that we were scared, but we held our positions and waited for the signal from Chris. When the boat was a bit over one hundred yards away we started firing every weapon we had above their heads. We weren't trying to hit them we just wanted to send a clear message that we had lots of firepower that we weren't afraid to use. It didn't take long for an M16 clip and a bunch of carbine ammo swooshing over their heads to make them pull a U-turn and haul ass out of there.

Looking back on everything I don't regret becoming a professional bass fisherman or a fishing guide. The truth is that I love every minute of it. But the other truth in my life is that I would have been perfectly content to spend my entire career as a commercial fisherman. And that's what Chris and I had been working towards. We always worked as crewmen on big boats like the Blue Gillian; but when the mackerel season was over and the seas were rough, there was still opportunity to make some money fishing the shallows and the Indian River. So we slowly but surely built up a fishing fleet of our own. Chris built a big river flatty and my dad helped me buy a 24-foot Suncoast with a 350 Chevy inboard. We added a couple more Suncoast boats over the years and were set up properly to do just about everything we needed to do on the small-boat end of commercial fishing. We fished for a wide variety of species but mostly focused on pompano, mullet, sea trout, and spots.

Of course the best thing about fishing on the Indian River is that we got to go home and sleep in warm, dry, comfortable beds. The living quarters on the big commercial fishing boats leave a lot to be desired. I actually never thought much about it until I visited Mystic, Connecticut with my wife, K.C. I was excited to see the old commercial fishing vessels and whaling boats, and we had a chance to tour inside some of them. I remember K.C. being shocked at how small the bunks were. She said they looked like little bitty coffins. I nodded and told her that not much had changed for hundreds of years. I said the bunks in most of our boats were just like that. I explained that the vertical boards on each side of the "mattress" – the boards that gave them their coffin look – were there for a reason. Basically you slept with one shoulder against each board and wedged yourself in so that you wouldn't get thrown to the deck if the boat hit rough waters. And when it was really rough, you didn't sleep at all. You just held on for dear life.

In a perverse kind of way, the good news is that commercial fishermen often go two or three days without any sleep. They work straight through for 48 to 72 hours. The bad news, of course, is that the strain of that kind of effort breaks down the human body and the human spirit. It will make full-grown men – big, tough, hulking men – cry like babies. The brain and the body simply get overwhelmed. After busting your butt for 24 hours you become a zombie, a shell of the man you were before you stepped foot on the boat. It's like your body takes over and just goes through the motions; and that's a dangerous situation because your alertness and senses are seriously diminished. That's when most accidents and injuries happen. Reaction times double or triple, and people get hurt. And to top it off, everyone loses their patience and the nicest guys in the world turn into ornery SOBs. Everyone's agitated and the guys start yelling and cussing at each other, fights break out, and threats of eternal damnation and revenge are tossed about like "Hallelujahs" at a revival meeting. But once the job is done and everyone's back on shore, everything is forgotten and forgiven. The guys toss back a couple of beers together, hug their wives and girlfriends, and try to rest up for the next job.

Aside from the physical hardships of commercial fishing, the job takes a heavy toll on personal relationships. It's difficult to have a wife or girlfriend when you're away for weeks at a time; and then, when you're back on shore, you're dead-tired. I once had a girlfriend break up with me because she couldn't deal with my schedule. I was really broken up about it and was telling another crewman how much I missed her. He was an older Cajun fisherman from Louisiana and he just shook his head and said, "Let me tell you something, boy. You can have a whiskey for a friend and you can have a dog for a friend. But when you try to have a woman for a friend, you're gonna find yourself drunk talking to a dog." I laughed like crazy and, while I didn't stop missing my ex-girlfriend, his advice did put things in perspective.

I always thought there would be a next job, but the commercial fishing industry in Florida came to a grinding halt in the early 1990's. There were lots of reasons given for the ban on drift-net fishing but, in my mind, it all boils down to over-regulation of the industry and a shortsighted mindset. Generations of commercial fishermen were wiped out. All of the boats and equipment Chris and I had worked hard to accumulate were now next-to-worthless. But the worst part of the deal is the amount of knowledge that was lost. All the tricks of the trade are dying along with the hardworking Americans who risked their lives to help feed our nation.

It's a sad chapter in our national history, but I could see it was history and I had to move on with the rest of my life.

Chapter 5

The Fisherman's Best Friend

On land, a dog is man's undisputed best friend. On the water, man's best friend is the dolphin – the magnificent sea mammal that is one of the smartest animals on the planet. Despite their cute appearance and playful attitude, dolphins can be very aggressive and, if provoked, quite vicious.

My first lasting memory of dolphins dates back to my first year on South Hutchinson Island. I was fishing for ribbonfish on the Indian River. Ribbonfish are really unusual looking and fun to catch. They're long and skinny. They can grow to about four-feet long, but they're only three or four inches wide, paper thin, and they sparkle and shine like a piece of chrome. They've also got incredibly sharp teeth like a barracuda, so you have to be very careful with them. I was fishing from the shore with a buddy when all of a sudden the water started boiling about twenty yards away. We jumped back not knowing what was going on, and then we spotted a team of dolphins ganging up on a shark. The shark was about four-feet long, either a black tip or a sand shark, and these dolphins were beating the snot out of it. Once they had finished killing the shark, the dolphins decided to have some fun. So for the next fifteen to twenty minutes the dolphins did a pretty good impression of the Harlem Globetrotters' "Sweet Georgia Brown" routine and passed that shark back and forth. They would toss it a couple of feet in the air, catch it and then flip it along to the next dolphin. It was an amazing thing to watch, and it was my first lesson in the no-love-lost relationship between dolphins and sharks.

It surprises most people to learn that cute little Flipper's relatives are at the top of the marine food chain with few natural enemies. They are also very social creatures who tend to live in pods of a dozen or more animals. While scientists don't understand exactly how dolphins communicate, there is no question that they have a relatively complex communications system consisting of a wide variety of clicking and whistling sounds. They are also empathetic beings and have been seen bringing injured members of their pod to the water's surface to breathe. And there have been many stories – both legendary and documented – of dolphins helping swimmers and fishermen. I probably would have doubted those stories had I not experienced the generous assistance of dolphins for myself.

Fact of the matter is, when I was working as a commercial drift-net fisherman, I counted one particular group of dolphins among my very best and most important friends. These guys (and probably gals since it's hard to tell the genders apart) were gigantic and I got to know them by sight. I knew them by their distinctive speckles and markings; and while I like to believe they knew me by sight as well, I think it's more likely they recognized the sound of our motors. Every boat engine has a different tone and dolphins have acute hearing that is many times more sensitive than humans'. And so when we were drift-net fishing for kingfish, the same group of dolphins would accompany us and swim up and down the cork line protecting our nets. I can't overstate how important this was – as well as the fact that the dolphins knew exactly what they were doing. Keep in mind that we would be drifting a net that was two miles long and 40-feet deep. This huge net is catching tons of kingfish. Well, kingfish look like pieces of chrome when they're hanging in the net, and they flash like a beacon to any shark within miles. When the sharks arrived they would tear the net to shreds, poking holes you could drive a semi through. But that wouldn't happen when the dolphins were around. I don't think dolphins are afraid of anything, but they're certainly not afraid of sharks. It's actually the opposite. Sharks are afraid of dolphins. Over time dolphins have learned how to ram a shark in the gills and knock him breathless and senseless. Remember that dolphins weigh almost 1000 pounds and can swim in bursts of speed up to 25 miles per hour. Put it all together and it's a powerful weapon that teaches sharks to keep their distance.

The dolphins helped us survive, and we rewarded them for their help. As we pulled up the net, we'd usually catch a bunch of bonitos that weren't worth much at the fish markets. So we'd take some of these bonitos, which might weigh 15 to 20 pounds each, and hang them over the side and watch a dolphin swim up and take it right out of our hands. We'd feed the dolphins like that just about every morning. We did it out of respect and appreciation for their help. Whenever you're out fishing on the open seas, you always feel that your fellow crewmembers are like family. You depend on each other to succeed. The dolphins were part of our extended family. And they knew they were helping us and they appreciated the way we helped them. There is no mistaking the way a dolphin rolls up on his side and looks at you. He's not looking at anything but your eyes, and he knows what's going on. It's like he's thinking, "Hey, we're good friends here. You scratch my back and I'll scratch yours."

And that's really how I view my relationship with every animal. All of God's creatures are here for a reason. We each bring something different to the table and it's pretty simple for all of us to live in harmony.

And just to make it clear to the anti-hunting PETA types, there is no contradiction in my belief that we need to live in harmony with the animals we hunt and fish. Animals are an important food source for the human race. That's been true since the dawn of creation and it will be true till the end of time. Hunting and fishing are key parts of the natural balance and the cycle of life. Death is a part of life. Hunters and fishermen like myself believe that animals have a right to live comfortable lives in their natural habitat and, when it comes time to be harvested, to die with dignity and respect. That's how you define harmony.

Chapter 6

The Mother Lode

Every fisherman has a story about the whopper that got away. Interestingly, most fishermen feel closer to the fish they missed than the ones they caught. Not so with commercial fishermen. They focus on their biggest and best catches, and my biggest catch was a doozy.

It was nearing the end of mackerel season off the coast of Florida. There was a spotter pilot that was flying around checking out schools of fish, and he reported seeing a gigantic school that stretched from Cape Canaveral all the way to Palm Beach. Chris and I set sail from Fort Pierce and headed north into the Atlantic. And we were not alone by any means. There were close to 100 commercial fishing boats in this part of Florida, and everyone had heard about this monster school and was out on the water looking for it.

Lady Luck was on our side that day because the fish were staying in deeper water. Most of the big fishing boats used roller rigs and purse nets, and they couldn't set in deep water because of the way the nets are made. Purse nets – which are also called seine nets – are divided into thirds horizontally. They have heavy black nylon on the top and bottom sections, while the center section is made of monofilament netting which was transparent in the water. So when you made a big circle around the fish they would see the black shadow at the top and bottom, and then a clear patch in the middle that looked like an exit. The problem was that if your net was too narrow to hit the bottom, any deep-swimming fish would go right underneath it. That was the situation most of the other fishing boats faced that day, so instead of dropping nets they were patrolling the coast and waiting for the school to move into shallower waters so they could set their gear.

Chris and I didn't have to wait. Our net was perfect for the situation. We'd just built this net and had designed it to fish deeper than the norm. It could fish top to bottom in 85 feet of water. It wasn't especially long, only around 800 yards, but its depth was exactly what we needed that day. We found the school of fish that the pilot had talked about and we identified a good spot to drop the net. We threw the buoy and drove the boat – and the net behind it – in a circle, making sure that the ends of the net overlapped. When the ends overlap each other, you know you've got the fish surrounded. At this point you have to move fast before the sharks figure out that something's going on and try to get a free meal out of it. Basically, as long as the fish are still swimming you don't have to worry too much about sharks; but once the fish hit the net, the sharks sense an opportunity and will pounce.

It's really amazing how these nets work. Once you encircle the fish, you start to purse the net with heavy-duty rope that runs all the way around the top of the cork and threads through steel rings. The whole thing is attached to a hydraulic pulley and roller. When the net starts to come in it looks like a big star. Once the hydraulics squeeze down to a certain point, the fish will all of a sudden hit the net. And once the first few hit the net, they usually all hit it at the same time.

On this particular day, we had no idea how many fish we actually had in the net. We knew it was a big catch, but nothing could have prepared us for what we were about to experience. Chris was in the wheelhouse and I was in the back of the boat with the rest of the crew working the lines. As we were pursing down the top of the net, we could see the vibrations from the fish hitting the gear. The fish had hit the center part of the net so hard that they actually lifted the bottom lead line, which was in 85 feet of water, and brought it almost to the surface. We saw the biggest catch of our lives and a sight that was beyond human comprehension.

Once the fish powered the net to the surface, the whole thing collapsed and went to the bottom. We had never sunk a net before, but this net was sunk. The whole damn thing. Almost immediately the oil started coming off these fish and floated to the surface; and we knew we were about to face a serious situation with sharks. Several of our friends were in the area and they brought their boats over and started to circle our gear. They were churning up the water and revving their big diesel engines, and that usually spooks most of the sharks away.

We started to pull up the net and we hit fish right off the bat. Usually they come in patches and clumps – what most fishermen call a "jag of fish" coming over the top of the roller. But this was a solid mass of fish, and it just kept coming and coming and getting thicker and thicker. The whole crew was working as hard as we could to get this load of fish on board. We kept loading, packing and shoveling ice. The hold in the bottom of the boat held 10,000 pounds, and we filled that without making a dent in the catch. We had another hold with 10,000 pounds of ice, which we removed and replaced with fish. We loaded another 26,000 pounds on the deck and now we're sitting pretty low in the water. Chris started shouting at us to stop loading before we hit the point of no return.

The problem was that there was still a lot of net in the water and a whole lot more fish in the catch. Something had to give and we had to move fast. I went below deck into the cabin and found water coming up through the shower stall and the floorboards. What's supposed to happen when you take a shower is that the water goes down into a drain and gets pumped out the side of the boat. Because the boat was sitting so low, water was splashing onto the deck and cascading below. But the drainage system was overloaded and instead of pumping water out it was just pushing it back in. We all started running around the boat making cones out of the Styrofoam net corks and wedging them into the drain plugs and plugging up every hole we could find. The bilge pump was running wide open, but we weren't making much progress and we kept taking on water.

It started to get real scary and we decided to cut the gear. We cut the net free and that took a huge load off the back of the boat. One of our friends, who'd been helping to keep the sharks away, picked up the cut section of net and was able to load an additional 16,000 pounds of fish. It was a huge haul by any measure – but our work wasn't done by a long shot. We were in a dangerous situation. We were carrying 46,000 pounds of fish, and while our boat was big and made to handle a lot of weight, it was sitting as low as any of us had ever seen.

Chris was in the wheelhouse running the boat and I stood by the window talking to him. We agreed that he'd just go nice and easy and not try to push it. So we just started idling along, but even so we could feel the boat roll with every wave. We kept a close eye on the pile of fish on the deck to make sure it didn't shift. The whole time water was coming across the bow of the boat and washing across my feet. Chris and I were holding hands, saying prayers, and asking the good Lord to help us navigate home safely. The rest of the crew was making sure that we weren't taking on water anywhere else and checking that the pumps were working. We were monitoring everything we could and then we finally saw the Fort Pierce Inlet. Normally this would provide a sense of comfort, but the water was a lot rougher in the Inlet. Chris and I looked at each other and shook our heads. We were both thinking the same thing: if this thing rolls there's no way any of us will survive. With the amount of weight we were carrying, it would have created a vacuum of biblical proportions. Chris was being as careful as possible but the boat rolled a few times – once so badly that I thought it was all over for us.

After an intense twenty or thirty minutes, everything changed. We sailed into calm water and you could feel an immense sigh of release from every member of the crew. And then the celebration started. We had earned – and I mean *earned* – the biggest paycheck of our lives. Word of our huge catch had preceded us to the dock and there was a crowd of people waiting for us along with a tall stack of pizzas. We backed up to the conveyors, took some pictures of our haul, and then worked another 20 hours straight to get all the fish out of the boat and onto the conveyor belts. As we worked from the boat, the fish house crew was packing the fish in ice, putting them in 1000-pound crates and loading them up on semis, freezer trucks and cold trucks for shipment to New York and other markets.

I'm sure that none of the New Yorkers or Bostonians who ordered mackerel off a menu or bought some at a supermarket gave a moment's thought to the effort – and danger – involved in catching the fish. And that's okay. But the memory of that 46,000-pound haul, the muscles that ached for days afterward, and the terrifying moments when we didn't know if we'd make it back to shore will live with Chris, myself and the rest of the crew until our dying day.

Chapter 7

My Sense of *Sensei*

On weekend nights, when I wasn't out fishing, I worked as a bouncer at a local dance club, Frankie & Johnnie's. I'd been doing it for a while and knew how to handle myself and the occasional drugged-out or drunken partier. One night I saw this absolute maniac out on the dance floor. I kept an eye on him because I sensed he was going to be trouble. He was a lot older than me, and he was big and rowdy. He'd been showing off his butt throughout the evening, and he kept going onto the dance floor with a drink in his hand. The club owner came over and asked me to talk to the guy and see if I could get him to put his drink on a table.

I nodded and went over to talk to the good old boy. I said, "Excuse me, sir. Would you mind if I set your drink on a table? We don't want you to spill it on the dance floor and have people start slipping and sliding."

The guy barely glanced at me and told me to go screw myself – though he used a bit more graphic language. I backed off for a few seconds to see if he would do as I asked.

But he stayed on the dance floor shaking his butt and drinking from his glass.

I moved close up to him and said, with a firmer voice, "Sir, you have to take that drink off of the dance floor."

This time he looked me right in the eye and grinned. He said, "You want this drink? Well here it is!"

He swung the glass as hard as he could and tried to hit me across the face with it. Because of my martial arts training, I had quick reflexes and was able to block his arm so he missed me completely. That seemed to really infuriate him, so he charged me and swung a fist at my head. I kicked him in the chest, and he crashed over a table and onto the floor. I thought for sure he was down for the count, but he got right back up and came at me again. I squat-kicked him upside the head, and hit him so hard I practically scalped him. The kick ripped the skin above his ear, off the back of his neck and up the side of his head; and it flipped his hair up like a poor-fitting toupee.

A buddy of mine, Billy, a bad cat who's in prison right now, came over to assess the situation. Billy looked at the guy and said, "I don't think he's going to fight any more." Billy reached down and grabbed the guy by the belt. Now the guy on the floor weighed about 250 pounds, but Billy picked him up without a hint of exertion. Billy walked the guy through the double-doored entrance and threw him out into the parking lot.

Later that same night, another buddy, Scott, was hanging out after closing time and was helping us clean up and haul trash out back. Scott's girlfriend was one of our waitresses and also tended bar. She was washing glasses when one broke and cut her hand open. Scott asked me to ride to the emergency room with them and get her hand stitched up. So I drove to the hospital and it was mayhem in the emergency room. It was a Saturday night and there were people bleeding and moaning all over the place. Scott and I were walking towards the check-in desk when we saw the butt-shaking guy I'd decked back at the club. He was walking down the hallway with about three-quarters of his head covered in white bandages, almost like a turban. He saw Scott and me and started to run towards us. I was shaking my head and thinking, damn, I don't want to do this again. A couple of doctors and orderlies grabbed him and tried to hold him back. At the same time the hospital's security guard, who was a little bit of a thing and looked like he was pushing seventy years old, was trying to get in between the crazy guy and me. Scott tapped the security guard on the shoulder and suggested that he might not want to get involved in this. The doctors and orderlies finally got the guy calmed down and escorted him out of the hospital.

The whole thing should have ended right there, but no such luck. I kept hearing all kinds of rumors around town that this dude was going to beat the crap out of me and/or kill me. And I'd occasionally see him drive by the karate studio and glare at me or toss the bird. It was a lot of stupid stuff like that and I didn't take it too seriously.

But then I took a construction job at the Rock Road Prison. My first day on the job site, I was walking across the parking lot with my welding leathers, hard hat and lunch box, and guess who I see just ahead of me? I felt like puking. I mean I was already depressed. I'd just lost my commercial fishing career, and now I have to put up with this crap. It didn't seem fair. This was a good job on a big project that was going to last a year or so, and I couldn't afford to lose it.

So over the first few weeks, I'd bump into this guy every once in a while and we'd just do some bad staring at each other. It was obvious to everyone that there was some bad blood, and so my boss asked me if I had issues with this guy. I explained that I had no issues with him; he had an issue with me and supposedly wanted to kill me. He told me to just stay focused on the job. And that's what I tried to do,

The prison we were building was designed as an octagon. There was a control tower in the middle of the octagon so the guards could see all the prison cells and monitor any activity inside them. There was a main octagonal wall that circled the prison and served as the back wall of all the cells. For extra security, there was also a secondary wall that faced the outside world. The idea was that if a prisoner were somehow able to bust a hole in his cell wall, he'd still be trapped in a buffer zone between the two walls.

This buffer zone, which was only a few feet wide, also served as a pipe chase, and I was working back there doing some welding. One day I was walking through the pipe chase, dragging welding leads, when I saw my old nemesis coming towards me from the opposite direction. As far as I knew there was no one else in the pipe chase but me and him. I stopped walking and stood there for a moment. I realized that the pipe chase was so narrow that, in order for him to walk past me, we'd both have to turn sideways and rub chests. And that would be uncomfortable, to say the least, for both of us. I watched him pull a hammer out of his tool belt and swing it back and forth. I dropped the welding leads and removed my welding helmet.

I returned his glare and said, "I want to tell you right now that you better hold onto that thing really tight and make sure you know how to use it."

He shook his head like he was confused and said, "What are you talking about, man?"

"Well," I said, "if you're going to use that hammer on me, I want you to hold onto it real good because if I get it, I'm going to shove it up your ass sideways." (Please excuse my language, but those were my exact words.)

The guy said, "I heard you were a pretty bad cat, and I guess people were right."

I said, "Dude, I didn't do anything to you. I was doing my freaking job. But if you want to give me a bunch of crap because you were acting like an idiot, then I'm ready to go. You want to go, let's go." I paused for effect and then continued. "I never say I'll whip a man's butt, but I tell you one thing. Be prepared. It ain't going to be easy. It's gonna be ugly as hell."

The guy stood there for a minute – in shock, I think – and put his hammer back in the sheath. He said, "You know, you're right. I was an idiot and I asked for it. You and me have pretty good jobs here, so as far as I'm concerned let's put everything behind us."

He came over and extended his hand. "I don't want any problems with you," he said.

We shook hands and that was the end of another of the many bizarro adventures of my life.

But it was an adventure that serves as a good example of my approach to conflict and conflict resolution. I've always been strong and I've had a lot of training in martial arts. I can hold my own against men bigger and stronger that me, but I've never looked forward to or relished a fight. In accordance with the *sensei* training of martial arts, I believe that fighting should be the course of last resort. I won't back down from a fight, but I'll never instigate one. And – as was the case with the butt-shaking guy – I've found that most people, other than drunks, will back down when challenged or will see the logic in letting bygones be bygones. The best fights are the ones we don't have to fight.

Chapter 8

Landlubber

I grew up around water. I was educated on water. And I always assumed I'd spend my life working on water. But life has a way of playing dirty tricks on you, and just when Chris and I started experiencing some real success as commercial fishermen, the state of Florida instituted a ban on drift net fishing. That meant all the nets that we had built over the years, all the equipment we owned, and the boats we had worked so hard to purchase, finance, and maintain were now obsolete. Every dollar we'd earned had been plowed back into our commercial fishing business, and now our slate had been wiped clean. We had to start all over and pursue Plan B – except that neither one of us had ever seriously considered a Plan B.

I'd held a few land jobs as a kid, but when I turned 18 I realized I needed to line up an income source during the off-season when fishing turned slow. I hated the idea of working my butt off on a boat but not making decent money. So shortly after my eighteenth birthday, I headed over to a construction site right on the island where they were building condos. I didn't have any construction experience at all, but that didn't stop me from walking up to the first trailer I came across and saying, "Hey, guys, you need any help?" The response was, "Maybe. What kind of experience you got?" I said none and so they shook their heads and motioned for me to keep moving. I went to the next trailer and had the same conversation. Then I got mad.

The next stop was an electrician's trailer, and the boss asked me the same question about my experience. I said I had no experience and he said then he couldn't use me. I said, "Listen to me for a second. Just give me one minute of your time. I commercial fish for a living. I can outwork every friggin' guy on this job site. I can go three days without sleep. I can work like a mule. I can do anything you want me to do. You just point me in the direction of what you want done and I'll do it. I need to work. So whatever you got, I don't care." So the guy just stood there for a minute, looked me up and down, and said to come with him. He gave me a bunch of paperwork to fill out and told me I could start the next day.

So I showed up the next day and he handed me a five-gallon bucket. He told me to fill it with concrete mud and patch up the walls around the electrical boxes. A couple of days later, I was working on the second floor of a 16-floor building and patching up the balcony walls. All of a sudden I heard everyone screaming. I saw something fall through the air right in front of me and I heard a loud boom. And then I saw red liquid get sprayed all over the railing, the ceiling, and me. I knew right away it was blood. Human blood. One of guys working on the sixteenth floor had fallen off. He landed on the ground and literally exploded. I looked over the railing and I saw an image that would haunt anyone for the rest of his life. The guy had hit a concrete washout – where they hose down and scrub concrete trucks – and he had landed feet first. The impact had pushed his thighbones right through his hips and they were sticking out into the air. The impact had broken his jawbone and pushed in the front of his face. All his insides had been squeezed up so that his neck was the size of a five-gallon bucket and blood and guts were gushing through his mouth. The whole top of his head had popped off, and I was looking down into his skull. Not surprisingly, I went into shock and was a trembling and crying mess. There were two guys near me that I had just met. They were brothers – T-Bone and Greg – and they were big old black boys. They took me down to the local bar in their neighborhood and got me calmed down. Later they took me home and then they always watched out for me. We became good friends for years after that.

The next morning, when I arrived on that same job site, a bunch of OSHA officials and several patrolmen from the local sheriff's office were there to investigate the previous day's accident. The job was shut down, but I hung out in the parking lot waiting for the issue to sort itself out. I noticed people going in and out of the security trailer where the overnight guard stayed. I knew a lot of the guys went in there to smoke dope, but I couldn't imagine them doing that with the cops right there. Finally one of the guys called the sheriff over and told him to go into the trailer. The sheriff discovered that the security guard was deader than dirt. Seems he had been walking on the beach that morning and found a kilo of cocaine. He decided to share his good fortune with his buddies, so that's why they kept going in and out. The security guard stayed there the whole time and evidently snorted a line or two too many and died there right on the spot. So now the cops were all over the site and they shut the job down. I went home and told Chris what had happened and he said, "Dude, this is crazy crap. Come back on the boat."

So I did go back to commercial fishing; and like I

described earlier, it was an up-and-down career. When the drift net ban went into effect, I needed to get serious about finding another career. I had done some steel work, and learned the trade, during the fishing off-season to help pay bills; and I figured that was my best prospect for steady work. The Indian River County Correctional Facility in central Florida was building an addition, and they were looking for strong guys that wanted to learn how to weld. The construction company was Willo Products out of Decatur, Alabama. Willo specialized in the construction and renovation of prisons and jails. That meant everything they built, and everything we touched, was reinforced and then reinforced again – which meant we were working with the heaviest equipment and building materials known to man. Because of the way Willo builds octagonal prison pods, all the material had to be carried in by hand – all the cell fronts, steel doors, bullet-proof glass, locking mechanisms and everything else that goes into a state-of-the-art prison. The guys I worked with were some of the biggest and baddest cats I'd ever seen. They were mostly country boys from Alabama and they all had shoulders like linebackers. I'd been doing martial arts since I was a kid and I always kept myself in good shape, but I got real jacked after carrying steel all day, putting it in place, tacking it up, welding it, and the whole nine yards.

That first job lasted five or six months. By that point, I'd become friends with a lot of those old boys and they said they'd call me if they got another contract in Florida. I bounced around for a few months, but then Willo called and offered me a job on another prison project they were doing right in Fort Pierce. I talked about it with Chris, who was working on a sword fishing boat. He wanted me to join him, but I saw that he wasn't making much money and I decided to stick with the steel work. I was still living at home on the island and it ripped my heart out to have to commute across the water every day. I never thought I'd work permanently at a land job, and now that's exactly what I was doing. But it was a job. That's what I kept telling myself.

I ended up doing a couple of more jobs for Willo and then the general contractor asked me to stay on with his crew. This guy took a liking to me and said they'd put me up in a trailer right on the job site. It was an ideal set-up for me. I kept my bass boat right beside the trailer, and I'd fish some of the local lakes and ponds after work, and then I'd come back home and have supper. In return, I served as onsite security at night – so it was a win-win for everybody.

It was hard and dangerous work. I was there when one of the younger guys, about my age at the time, fell off scaffolding. He landed on his feet but that's where his good luck ended. There was some rebar jutting from a concrete slab, and the rebar pierced up between his rectum and spinal cord about a foot and a half. We tried to hold his body weight off the bar until the fire department and ambulance arrived. The fire captain and EMTs took one look at the guy and told us to ice the rebar so it would stay cool while they cut it from the concrete. There was no way they could have removed the bar from his body without losing him. They called in a helicopter to take him to a hospital and, miraculously to those of us who saw what had happened, the guy survived. The rebar hadn't injured his spinal cord so he wasn't paralyzed, but his intestines were torn up really bad and he had to go through the rest of his life with a colostomy bag.

One of scariest moments I experienced as a steelworker was when I was working on a project in Orlando. We had a crew of old union carpenters who had done most of the work on Disney World and Universal Studios. One of the carpenters was this little bitty guy in his late fifties or early sixties. He might have weighed 150 pounds soaking wet, but he was the nicest guy, a great carpenter and very smart. He was also a diabetic. This was the summertime and we were often working in 100-degree temperatures. The heat was taking a toll on everyone and an older diabetic like him should not have even been working, but he was. We were up on the deck setting precast concrete beams. The beams had a span of about four feet apart. You'd lay plywood between the beams, secure it with little metal clips, lay rebar and then they could pour concrete slabs. Well there were five or six of us working a couple of floors up. I was talking to one of the other carpenters when we both spotted the little guy shaking. He was having a full-blown diabetic seizure and he started folding up. He was just barely hanging on to the beam, and we knew it was a matter of seconds before he fell. Everybody got kind of panicked, trying to figure what to do. A couple of guys started to drop plywood boards across the beams so they could walk out to help him. As young as I was, I had seen a lot of crazy stuff in my life and didn't get scared by much – so I decided to let my martial arts training pay off. I focused and walked across the beams to where the older guy was struggling to hold on. I straddled the four-foot span and grabbed him by his tool belt. I picked him up with one arm, spun back around and carried him down the beam to the solid deck. The guys called an ambulance and got him to the hospital where he was held overnight and then released the next morning hardly the worse for wear.

From an employment standpoint, this was a very stable time in my life. I had a steady income and I worked for and around a lot of good people. But it was also a time of personal assessment. Now I freely admit that I'm not a terribly complex character, but I'd reached a point in my life where I had to make some decisions. Major decisions. I had just turned twenty-five and was seriously considering joining the pro bass fishing circuit. I had the sense to know that I wasn't quite ready; I still had a lot to learn, but I was hungry and ready to make the commitment.

There was another consideration as I hit the quarter-century mark. I wanted to try and get to know my father in a way that I could never accomplish by the occasional phone conversation.

Like I said, I worked for a great group of people and they were very supportive of my decision to move back to Ohio to learn to fish northern waters and to spend time with my dad. Fact is, they weren't just supportive they were also very generous. They gave me a few thousand dollars to help get me started, and the head superintendent's wife came down to the job site and gave me a haircut to make me a little more presentable. So I loaded my truck with everything I owned, hitched up my bass boat, and headed north to fish, make amends with my father, and begin the second quarter-century of my life in the same place I began the first.

MARK SHEPARD

Section Two:

One With Nature

Chapter 9

The Chill of the Hunt

Most of the time when I go hunting, I go home empty handed. It's not because I'm a bad shot, but rather because I usually choose not to take a shot. That's my number one rule whether hunting with a gun or bow – if you don't have a good shot, don't take it. Let the animal go rather than take a flop shot.

Hunting is about so much more than bag limits and trophy antlers. It's about the inner peace that comes with being one with nature.

Our life is so fast and furious that when you walk into the woods you can see how quiet and peaceful the whole world used to be. You can see our heritage as human beings and Americans. You can see how the pioneers lived. Those people worked hard to survive, but they were also surrounded by the majestic beauty of nature. The whole experience soothes the soul. It's true peace on earth.

From the moment I could walk, I preferred to be outdoors. I've always loved watching all of God's beautiful creatures in their natural habitat – whether it was the brightly colored fish I watched snorkeling as a little boy, the seabirds that tracked our commercial fishing boats, or the majestic elk and moose that roam the near-wilderness regions of our big-sky states. It's hard not to smile when you see these animals exploring their unique worlds, eating and playing with each other, and sometimes fighting for dominance or survival.

My buddy Larry Martgolio, who's been a biologist and ranger for the U.S. Forest Service and other organizations, describes his own experiences like this:

> *Every minute in the woods is great. There is always something interesting going on when deer are not in sight, which is about 99% of the time. The hours I've spent sitting in a tree stand were how I came to appreciate the hoots of sandhill cranes, the honking of geese, and the migrations of ducks and song birds. I vividly remember one day, just before dark, when I watched a pileated woodpecker land in a dogwood tree and eat 52 – because I counted – of its dogberry fruits before going to roost in a big tree and (I can only assume) fall into a food-induced coma.*

One of the first lessons every hunter should learn – and it's a lesson that can only be learned through close and patient observation – is that animals know the woods way better than we do. They notice every single thing that's out of the ordinary; and if they don't like or recognize what they see or hear, they'll be out of there like a shot from a cannon. And even if it doesn't spook them immediately, their senses will be raised and they'll be ready to boogie.

The slow and patient approach to hunting doesn't end after you've fired a shot and hit your target. In fact, that's probably the most important time to be patient to make sure you don't lose the animal. This is one of the hardest rules for newer hunters to follow. It's natural to want to celebrate when you've shot your first deer or hog, but you really need to stay calm, stay quiet, and stay where you are. When you shoot any kind of larger size game – whether from a tree stand or blind – don't move and don't start yelling or clapping. Just stay where you are for a good thirty minutes. That's right, thirty minutes. Even if you're confident that you hit the animal right in the heart, let him lie there for a while. It's an ethical thing because you never want to lose an animal. They are all precious. You want to give the animal time to lie down and allow him to die without any additional stress. When you do start to look for the animal, you do it quietly. You need to remember where the animal was when you shot it, and look for traces of his kick-off in the dirt and leaves. If you're using a bow, the next step is to look for the arrow. The arrow is the most important factor in bow hunting because it can tell you the whole story of your shot. If the arrow is covered with bright red blood, you know there was a lot of oxygen in the blood. That means you made a good hit, probably in the heart, and the animal would have died very quickly. If the arrow has blood that's kind of pinkish in color with foam and bubbles on it, then you know you hit a lung. That's another good hit that will kill the animal in a very short time. Both these types of hits will leave a good blood trail to follow.

If you make a bad shot and the animal doesn't bleed much, then the only way to trail him is by hoof marks. And if you're hunting in the fall, when most deer seasons run, there will probably be leaves on the ground and you'll have a really hard time trying to find a hoof trail. Hoof marks can disappear very quickly and you can lose a beautiful animal. It may sound counterintuitive, but this is exactly why it's so important to let the animal stay alone for a while after shooting him. It's like insurance. If you make a bad hit on a deer, he might run 50 or 100 yards and then bed down in leaves. The leaves will stick to the wound and slow the bleeding. So if you track him down and show up too soon while the deer is still alive, he's liable to jump up and take off. And because the wound is caked up with dirt and leaves, the bleeding will be slowed or eliminated. You'll end up with no trail to follow and you'll have lost him. And that is one sad day at the office. (One way to avoid losing an animal that isn't bleeding very much or is dripping blood on autumn leaves where it's tough to see is to carry a small bottle of peroxide. That way if you see something that might be blood, you can just mist it with the peroxide and watch if it bubbles. If it does, it's blood.)

If you find the arrow and it has really dark blood on it, you might have hit him in the liver or kidneys. That means you made a good vital shot and the animal is definitely going to die, but let him sit for a couple of hours before you track down his body. If the arrow smells like gut – like the contents of stomach – or smells like crap, you've made a terrible shot and hit the animal in the stomach. Leave him alone for 12 hours or even wait 24 hours because he won't wander off more than 100 yards if you let him die in peace. Those are the shots – whether by gun or arrow – you don't want to make. The animal will take a longer time to die, and the meat will be tainted because those stomach and intestinal acids spread through the animal very quickly. But you still don't want to waste that animal. The meat will still be edible. It won't be the finest tasting meat but it's perfectly fine for hamburgers or sausages. With this kind of hit, you'll lose the inside tenderloins and shoulders, but the hams and backstraps should be in good shape.

The key thing is to never push an animal. I've had some of the most perfect shots and still followed this advice. I once had a whole herd of does come up upon me. And I had a powerhouse of a bow with a mechanical broadhead arrow that opened up to more than three inches in diameter. There was one doe in the group that was real old – its back was swaying; she was silver-nosed; and she was gigantic. You could tell she didn't have much time left on her schedule and I decided to take her. She gave me the perfect opportunity and I hit her right in the heart. When I field-dressed her later, I saw that the arrow had actually split her heart right in half. When I shot her, she moved about ten yards and then fell down dead. But even though she was clearly dead, I still gave her a half hour before coming down from my stand. Because I shot her with an arrow and she went down so fast, the other deer weren't spooked at all. They kept grazing and going about their normal business and then eventually wandered off. If I had jumped down right away after shooting the doe, I would have spooked the herd and made them all nervous and crazy for no good reason.

Of course, everything I'm preaching today is a result of what I've learned over the forty-plus years of my life. I started out like every other hunter and outdoorsman – way too confident in my own abilities and knowledge level. I remember my first hunting season up in Ohio. I'd been training with my bow all summer and felt like I was shooting really well. A farmer near my dad's house invited me to hunt his land. He walked me through the property and showed me all the game trails. Back in the woods I found a perfect tree for my stand where I could see a bunch of trails. So I was getting excited and the opportunity finally arrived for my first hunting adventure. Now it gets a lot colder in Ohio than I was used to in Florida, and some of my working buddies told me it was going to be way too cold for hunting. I brushed aside their concerns because it was the only day I had off from work. I figured I'd just dress warm and I'd be fine. Truth of the matter was that I didn't have a lot of winter clothing, but I got up that morning and put on the heaviest clothes I had. The sun wasn't up yet when I got out of the truck, and it was bone-chilling cold outside. I kind of knew I was gonna be in trouble; but I figured I'd be generating a lot of body heat by carrying my backpack, tree stand and bow. I also fooled myself into thinking that I could always warm myself up by walking faster. Not the smartest decision I've ever made. Anyway I made it to my tree fairly comfortably, climbed up and got myself situated. Well it wasn't more than twenty minutes later that I started getting really cold. Then the sun came up and I figured that would warm me up a bit, but no such luck. It wasn't much longer before I couldn't feel my feet anymore, and then they were tingling and stinging so bad that I could hardly move. And I was getting scared. This was at a time when I was in the best shape of my life. I was tough, did a lot of martial arts and, basically, I could eat a bucket of rusty nails and poop an I-beam. But none of that mattered that morning. I knew I had to get down from the stand and get warmed up as soon as possible, but every movement hurt. I slowly made my way down the tree and stood on the bottom platform which was only about a foot off the ground. I jumped off the platform to the ground and it felt like I had stepped off a high diving board and landed on concrete. The pain was incredible and I stumbled my way back to the car. I came damn close to getting frostbite that day and learned never again to test Mother Nature. I invested in some better hunting clothes and learned that you can comfortably go out in the woods and enjoy just about any weather condition. You just need to be smart about it.

And that really gets to the heart of how to make the most of every hunting experience. Be smart. You want to challenge yourself, but you never want to put yourself in danger. The most peaceful times I've ever spent have been in the woods holding a rifle or bow, appreciating nature, and celebrating our human heritage as hunters.

Chapter 10

The Dearest Of Animals

I love every single one of God's creatures. I'll swerve my car to avoid hitting a snake or squirrel. I can't pass a dog without bending down to scratch its ears and stroke its fur. I can spend hours on end watching dolphins splash in the ocean, and I still marvel at the prehistoric bodies of gators and crocs.

But my favorite animal by far is the whitetail deer. I love the way it prances in the woods. I love the way does protect their fawns and the way bucks fight for dominance. I love the alertness of deer and the challenge that creates for us hunters. And I love the way venison tastes.

Now I know there are anti-hunting folk out there who think this is a huge contradiction. I mean how can you love an animal and proceed to shoot it? My response is simple: How can you love deer and allow them to over-populate an area to the point of starvation and rampant disease? But more about that later. Let me tell you about my first deer.

It's very rare for a first kiss to be the best kiss you ever experienced. And it's equally rare for your first harvested deer to rank among the best hunting experiences of your life, but that's the truth in my case.

It was late fall in Ohio and the deer hunting season was almost over. It was still the middle of the night and sunrise was a long way off, so it was damn near pitch black. I didn't want to spook any of the deer that I knew were bedded down in the woods, so my plan was to walk through the center of a large cornfield that was bordered by the woods and a county road. I was carrying my tree stand on my back like a backpack, and I had my bow and a little bitty flashlight. And did I mention that it was freezing cold out with icy rain and sleet? Anyway, I'm walking through the cornfield and I knew it wasn't going to be an easy hike, but I don't think I realized just how hard it would actually be. My boots were getting packed with mud, picking up what felt like two or three pounds of slop with every step. But I was in really good shape and I was moving along at a pretty good pace. I got about three-quarters of the way through this cornfield, when I started hearing noises that I didn't really recognize and couldn't quite tell where they were coming from. I was all by myself with no one else around for miles. And while I wouldn't quite say that I have nerves of steel, I don't scare easily; but I was still new to this hunting thing and I was a little nervous about all the things I didn't know. I kept trudging ahead and then all of a sudden I saw a flash of gray – kind of like a helicopter – pop up right in front of me and then proceed to hit me in the face. I fell backward and I felt my whole life flash in front of my eyes. I just about pooped a purple Twinkie and I was thinking this is it. This is the big one. So I was lying on the ground with sleet slapping against my face and this helicopter thing fluttering overhead, and then it occurred to me that I'd been hit by a bird. I didn't know what kind of bird, but I knew I'd been attacked by some kind of man-eating killer bird. (Later, when I told this story to friends and suffered through their jokes and laughter at my expense, I learned that the bird was a grouse that nests on the ground and does indeed take off like a helicopter.)

When I realized it was just a bird that had scared me half to death, I started to laugh at myself and tried to get up. Well the tree stand I was carrying on my back was slammed into the mud and I wasn't going anywhere as long as I was attached to it. I maneuvered out of the straps and rolled face down into the mud so I could push up to my knees and, eventually, stand up. I was covered with mud and muck, but I got myself back together again and told myself the rest of the day was going to be great 'cause it couldn't get any worse.

So I continued on to the area where I had planned to hunt and put the tree stand in place. It was still dark, with no moonlight. The sleet was still coming down and if I turned off the flashlight I literally couldn't see my hand right in front of my face. I examined my bow and tried to remove as much mud as possible. I took a deep breath and settled into my hunting zone.

One thing I've noticed over all the years I've been hunting is that once you get up into your tree stand you take on a whole different mindset. I always feel safe up there – no matter how dark or stormy. The way I figure it is that even if there was a bear who took an interest in me and tried to climb the tree to reach me, I could just poke him in the nose with an arrow and he'd hightail it out of there. So I was in my tree stand feeling nice and relaxed, and the sun was starting to light up the horizon. It was turning into a beautiful morning – a little hazy but you could see a long way and there were birds flying and chirping everywhere.

And then I looked across the street and saw him. The Godzilla of deer. I mean this was a huge, full-grown, gorgeous animal with a spectacular rack. And close by him was a goofy-horned buck.

Now let me digress. When you have a lot of deer in one area that aren't being harvested by hunters or killed by predators, you often have the dominant buck breeding with its own daughters. This in-breeding often results in deformities. I've seen deer with five legs and I once shot a deer that had an antler growing right above its eye and the eye was completely shut. In addition to genetics, goofy horns can also result from an injury. A deer might get hit by a car or breaks a leg and that injury – somewhere else in their body far away from their horns – can affect antler growth. And interestingly, the goofy horns usually grow on the side opposite from where the injury was. A while back I shot a really big buck that I'd been watching for about three years while waiting for a clear opportunity to get him. After I harvested him I noticed that his rack was much smaller than usual and one of the sides was curved way in. I saw that his jaw had been broken and I learned later that he had been hit by a car. This deer was 300 pounds, one of the biggest I've ever harvested, and in perfect physical health other than the goofy horns. That broken jawbone was making his horns grow goofy. Now I'm not a vet or a biologist, so I don't know if it's a neurological thing – but I do know that injuries play a role in why some deer have goofy horns.

So getting back to my story, this goofy-horned deer was hanging around near the Godzilla buck. And from where I was up in my tree stand, the goofy-horned deer looked mature, healthy and full-bodied; but his rack was just a jumble of horns going in every which direction. He was walking close to the big buck, and the big boy seemed to have had enough of the goofy-horned one. Keep in mind that bucks are vicious animals. They will fight to the death, and their power is almost incomprehensible.

So all of a sudden the big buck just reared back and knocked the snot out of the goofy-horned deer. The goofy-horned deer got disoriented, started running in a circle and then headed towards the fence. He jumped over the fence in a powerful leap and crossed the road. He then jumped the second fence and started running along the fence line towards me.

And all the while I'm thinking, thank you Lord, this is absolutely perfect.

I mean I couldn't have planned it any better. That big buck was going to chase this goofy-horned one and I was going to get the deer of a lifetime. Right there, right now. I was counting my coins long before I ever got paid and high-fiving myself in celebration of finally getting my first deer.

And then just like I'd imagined it in my mind, he started coming. The big buck came charging. He jumped over the first fence and then paused in the middle of the road. Now this road had a sharp curve and I could hear the truck before I saw it. The big buck seemed to hear it also, but he didn't know what to do. At the very last moment he tried to take off, but his hooves had trouble getting traction on the asphalt. The truck plowed into him and killed him instantly. The truck didn't do much better, and the driver hopped out of the cab and started cussing and hollering at the damage to his truck.

And me? I was just sick to my stomach. This couldn't be. No one could be this unlucky.

The goofy-horned buck must have also been goofy-brained because he just stood there watching the whole thing unfold. At this point, he was directly between me and the truck and the dead buck. I guess he figured he was out of danger so he started walking in my direction. In my head I was doing some quick calculations. The season was almost over and I was not going to have many more chances to land me a deer. So I decided to take this guy and, as a side benefit, make sure he didn't pass along his defective genes. The goofy-horned deer positioned himself right in front of me. I took a bead on him. I let the arrow fly, hit him perfectly, and he went down in a matter of seconds. And that, ladies and gentlemen, was my first deer. The horns were nothing to be proud of, and it wasn't an exceptionally glorious hunting experience – but it made for one hell of a memory.

Afterwards I asked around whether anyone had heard about a deer killed on the road up in Somerville and told them my story of woe. And they said, "Yeah that was a big old buck, at least 12 points," and they'd laugh at my misfortune and rub it in every chance they could.

Deer hunting got a lot better for me after that first harvest. I learned what I was doing wrong, got calmer and more patient. The next year another farmer invited me to hunt his land. This farm had a lot of history. There were a couple of hand-dug wells from the seventeen- and eighteen-hundreds and graveyards from the same period. One time I was walking on a creek bottom that ran right through the middle of a giant cornfield. I was walking through a big tangle of briars, vines and scrub trees and I felt myself kick a big rock. I looked down and saw it was a tombstone. I start looking more closely and I saw tombstones all around me. They were broken and crumbling and all dated back almost two hundred years. I started reading the inscriptions and tried to visualize the babies, kids, couples and old people buried beneath my shoes. It was all very fascinating stuff. My permanent tree stand was set up close by so I got a chance to revisit this area very frequently.

One of the hunting memories that most stands out in my mind occurred when I was hunting this particular farm. I knew this area had a very large and active deer population, which was why the farmer had asked me to thin the herd. But nothing could have prepared me for the experience of watching, with zero exaggeration, forty-seven deer walk right in front of me during a single morning. And you know what? I didn't take a shot. I just settled back and watched these beautiful creatures go about their daily lives in one of the prettiest areas I've ever hunted.

I'm not the only one who has taken a more patient approach to hunting whitetail. It used to be that hunters would take their place, spot a deer, say "Oh my gosh, a deer!" and shoot the first deer they saw. Nowadays, there's a lot more understanding of and appreciation for the ways of the woods. And that understanding translates into being more patient and becoming a better hunter. The biggest trick to getting a good deer – a big deer – is to let one or more deer walk by. I always tell new hunters that if you're in a tree stand or behind a blind and you see a couple of does, let them walk by. You can be pretty confident that there's a big buck tailing them in the woods. And that big deer is smart. He knows that if those does can walk through the area safely, it's safe for him as well. That's how you make a good harvest.

Every single hunt for whitetail is an adventure, especially when you get up real close and personal to them. I've been in ground blinds where a whitetail would stick its nose right up to the screen, no more than two feet from you on the other side of the screen, and they'll snort at you. That's actually one of the biggest thrills and the thing that always makes me smile. Deer snort a lot, especially when they get upset. They do it to alert the other deer that something's not right. I remember a number of times when I was walking through the woods towards a tree stand, too dark to see anything but whatever the flashlight was shining on, and suddenly a deer jumped up and snorted at me. I can promise that a deer snort will get your attention real fast. And the first time you hear it, when you're first learning to hunt and getting used to going into the woods at night, a deer snort will scare the living crap out of you.

It might surprise you that deer would allow a hunter to get so close. Deer do have a great sense of smell, but it's all based on the wind. So if you're downwind, they may not notice you until you're only yards apart. The direction of the wind also helps determine where and how you'll be hunting that day. Bow hunters especially have to pay close attention to the wind because wind will get you busted faster than anything out there. So if you're going to be hunting a particular patch of woods you might have three locations – a tree stand, a blind and another tree stand – and you'll choose which to use on any given day based on which way the wind is blowing. You always want to be on the downwind side of where the deer are likely to be traveling.

One of my closest encounters with deer was also one of the most violent displays I've ever seen. I'm sure you know that a dominant buck will mark out his territory and defend it aggressively. If another buck wanders in to work the area, he's going to have a fight on his hands. And that's exactly what I happened upon while hiking through some Ohio woods one day. I was walking with my girlfriend when I heard branches snapping and then saw two big bucks come hurtling right at us. We positioned ourselves tightly between two pine trees and watched in fear and awe as these two giant bucks went at each with pure hate. They got as close as two or three feet from us but paid us absolutely no attention. They couldn't have cared less if there was a rock concert going on. These boys were focused on beating each other to the ground and, ideally, putting the other in his grave. It was truly amazing to see the massive power of these two animals going full bore at each other right in front of me. Fur was flying, blood was spouting from open wounds, and antlers were clanking against each other like two freight trains colliding. It was both terrifying and beautiful, and it was a scene I'll never forget.

And it's not just the bucks that enjoy a good fight. Does can go at it just as viciously. I've seen does rear up on their hind legs and box each other like a pair of welterweights. They don't have the power of bucks nor the built-in weapon of antlers, but does will fight hard if they feel threatened.

So deer kill deer and hunters kill deer. But you know what? More deer are killed by cars than by hunters. And it's not me saying that – it's a large number of wildlife biologists and researchers. There was a study done up in Utah that amazed me and points to the magnitude of the problem. The Utah Division of Wildlife Resources (UDWR) studied a twenty-two mile stretch of highway. In 2009, UDWR personnel removed 132 dead deer from the highway. In 2010, they removed 121. Those numbers equate to six deer per mile per year. Unfortunately, those numbers don't tell the whole story. No one knows how many more deer were hit by cars and wandered away, injured and suffering, to die in the woods. Some research studies have estimated that the number of deer collected from roads and highways represents less than fifty percent of the number of deer actually hit and killed by cars. There have even been some studies that suggest the number of deer found on roads could equal less than 12 percent of the total number hit and killed by cars.

That's bad – but here's what's worse. Cars are killing the deer that are most important to maintaining a healthy and diverse herd – the does and fawns. Hunters mostly take bucks. That's the prized harvest. But cars don't choose the deer they kill; they kill whatever jumps out in front of them.

It's sad. As a nation, we need to come up with a plan to better protect our wildlife – especially our deer in more populated urban and suburban areas. In the interim, everyone can make a difference. The first step is to simply be more aware when driving. Deer eyes glow in the night. They look like two little reflectors and that's what people should look for when they're driving on a dark road at night. Secondly, if a deer does run across the road in front of you, wait a few moments before continuing to drive. Sometimes a deer will run across the road and there'll be a fence or other obstruction blocking it. The deer will often panic, turn on a dime and come right back at you. Remember that the deer doesn't know what's going on. All he sees are the bright lights of the car blinding him. He knows where he was before, when he felt safe, and will try to go back there again – right into the road right in front of you. So anytime you see a deer jump in front of you, please slow down and wait for the whole deal to unfold. The life you save may be your own as well as the deer's.

Chapter 11

Hog Heaven and Hell

Pigs have a special place in the heart of most Americans. We grew up with "The Three Little Pigs," Porky Pig, Miss Piggy, and Piglet of "Winnie the Pooh" fame. We think about pigs as cute domesticated animals, but there's a dark side to the "other white meat" that few of us know or understand. At least four million wild pigs are spreading disease and ruining property in more than thirty-nine states, and they'll probably hit all forty-eight continental states in our lifetimes.

That's why it's open season on hog hunting in most states – with any kind of weapon and no bag limit – and why I'm an avid hunter of wild sows and boars. I'm also an avid eater of the hogs I harvest. It's one of the best tasting meats I've ever had. When I travel around and talk to people about hunting, they always ask what wild hogs taste like. The answer is simple—they taste just like the plastic-wrapped pork you buy in the supermarket only better. Wild hogs aren't pumped up with chemicals, steroids, and antibiotics; they're also leaner with much less fat, so they're actually healthier for you.

My first hunt for wild hogs didn't quite turn out like

I'd imagined. My brother and I were equipped with compound bows, and we were hunting in the Three Lakes Wildlife Management Area, part of the Kissimmee Prairie in central Florida. We took different positions on opposite sides of a cabbage palm hammock. There was nothing doing for a good long while, and I was relaxing against an old abandoned fence. There wasn't much daylight left and it was kind of eerie quiet. All of a sudden a pig lets off a screaming squeal, and I hear it take off like a cannonball rampaging through the cabbage palm. I jumped up and started to run back to where Chris was. He was all kinds of excited; and I shouted, "Did you get one?" He nodded up and down like a crazed bobble-head doll and said, "Yep, I shot a giant hog." We ran over to where Chris had shot the hog and found the arrow laying on the ground. We picked it up and expected to see some blood and guts on the arrowhead, but there was nothing but the tiniest trace of fat on the chisel-point blade. There was no blood trail and absolutely no trace of the hog.

One of our buddies came over when he heard the commotion and asked whether it was a big hog. Chris nodded. "Just about the biggest one I've ever seen," he said.

"Well that explains it," our friend said. "You must have hit the shield."

We were brand new to hog hunting and really didn't know much about the biology of pigs, but we both shook our heads and said something to the effect that "Hogs don't have shields."

"Sure they do," he said. "They grow shields up on their front shoulders to help protect them when fighting."

Chris and I found that hard to believe, but our friend went on to explain that hogs rub up against trees and build up what are essentially huge calluses. Once I started harvesting hogs and dressing them, I understood exactly what he was talking about. Skinning a pig can be like trying to peel off a layer of three-quarter-inch plywood up there by the front shoulders. And without exaggeration, that leather can be two or three inches thick. I've harvested some pigs over the years that had gashes three or four inches long and a good two inches deep from when they'd been sliced by another boar's tusk. Those gashes usually had hardly any blood in them; they just healed up and scarred.

Most people don't realize how dangerous and ferocious wild hogs can be. Boars have four tusks, two that grow from the upper jaw and two larger ones from the lower. They sharpen the lower tusks – which serve as their attack weapons – by rubbing them against the upper. The lower tusks curve upwards and can inflict serious wounds on their victim's soft tissue areas around the stomach and groin.

Hogs fight for dominance. The boars in particular will fight over sows in heat. When you're in an area like the Everglades with a big population of hogs, you can hear them fighting just about every day. Hogs let out bone-chilling squeals when they get to fighting and you can hear them way off in the distance.

Size matters in the hog hierarchy. The smaller boars don't even try to mess with the big boys, and they won't mate with a sow unless there are no other boars around. So when you shoot a smaller boar – let's say under 200 pounds – they usually don't have the scars and wounds you see on the bigger boys because they stay away from the action. The big boars, on the other hand, are sometimes so cut up that they look like they got into a fight with a chain saw. I've seen some that literally look like their face got caught on fire and someone tried to put it out with an ice pick.

Most hog aggression is directed at other hogs, but they will attack people. And it's not just the boars. Sows will attack if you get between them and their babies, and most any hog will attack if it feels cornered or senses it has nowhere else to go. As wild animals go, hogs are not especially aggressive; so if they can get away from you they will. But if you corner one, they will stand their ground and they will charge.

I personally had a close encounter with a set of massive tusks that I'll never forget. And it happened because hogs don't see or hear very well. That means it's easy to surprise them. I was hunting on a ranch up in Labelle, Florida. I had set myself up in a tree stand but, after a while, decided to get down from the stand and walk along a sandy road towards a scrub oak hammock. I came around a turn and found three huge hogs staring at me. They were only about 20 yards from me and I had nowhere to go. I had cabbage palm hammock on both sides of me, plus a stand of scrub oaks that were way too small to even think about climbing. I had no choice but to stand my ground. Fortunately I had a big compound bow in my hand with an 80-pound draw. The middle hog was a huge boar and he charged me at full speed. Instinct took over and I drew back on the bow. I let the arrow fly and hit him right in the neck. The arrow went right through him like a shish kabob skewer. The other two hogs ran off to my side, but that middle hog kept charging. The arrow may have slowed him down a bit but his little brain was still focused on killing me. When the boar got to about two yards of me, I jumped to the side and he flew right past without touching me. And that's the trick. If you ever do get charged by a hog, wait till the last second and step aside. Hogs charge with their heads and tusks low to the ground, and they can't turn very well. In reality, you could jump right over a charging hog – but you damn well better not make a mistake because one false move and you'll get hooked.

***

I've harvested a lot of hogs over the years. I've also lost a lot and I was determined to figure out why. About five years ago my buddy, Jerry, and I were invited by a local farmer to hunt his property and thin out the hog population that was destroying everything. We decided to use the opportunity to learn as much as we could about hogs – their habits and biology – and the keys to successful hog hunting.

We were hunting with bows and started experimenting with different arrow tips. We used broadheads and mechanical broadheads, but felt the results were inconsistent. Ultimately we found that fixed blades without chisel tips worked best. The arrow went all the way through the animal and made finding the pig easy.

One thing I learned during this period was the importance of understanding the anatomy of the animal you're hunting. I'll never forget shooting two hogs straight through the chest, not being able to track or find them, and then seeing them again at their feeders a short time later. I wrote it off as one of those unlucky shots that goes straight through the animal but doesn't seriously hurt him. Good news for the pig but bad news for me. Because of these experiences, I started paying closer attention when I was butchering and cleaning the hogs I'd harvested. I saw that their lungs sat high up in their chest, their spine was up near their shoulder blades just like in a deer, and their heart sat way down low at the bottom of the chest between their front legs. And in between their heart and lungs is this area of non-vital organs that seemed to be a magnet for my arrows.

Once we better understood a hog's anatomy, we started zeroing in on the lowest section of their chest and our success rate soared. We'd shoot an arrow straight through the hog's heart and it would look like blood shooting out of a garden hose; and the hog wouldn't move more than 10 or 20 yards before folding up on the ground. This information also led me to prefer to hunt hogs from a ground blind rather than a tree stand. At ground level you're shooting straight into the side where the heart and lungs are rather than shooting down from a tree stand at a more awkward angle.

I also prefer to hunt hogs with a bow. It's a very stealthy way of hunting that I find more challenging. I like the fact that bows are quiet and you don't disturb any other animals. Plus, with a bow, you can often take more than one shot because hogs won't necessarily disperse when one of their buddies goes down or takes off.

For all the hog hunting I've done, however, I've never shot a momma sow – a sow that is pregnant or still caring for her babies. The idea of killing a momma sow in her natural habitat and letting her babies starve to death or have to fend off predators by themselves just makes me cringe. I won't do it – no way, no how. It's not something any ethical hunter would do.

**

Like I said at the beginning of this chapter, most states have open season on the hunting of wild hogs. The state of Missouri has publicly urged its 500,000 licensed deer hunters to target wild hogs; and Michigan has issued a "shoot on sight" order to its hunters. The reasons are abundantly clear. Wild hogs can grow to more than 300 pounds and their massive bodies and broad snouts can uproot an entire residential lawn or golf course fairway overnight. It'll look like someone went through with a plow. They flip the sod or grass over, knock the dirt off and eat the roots. And that's an important fact – they don't actually eat the grass. They eat the roots of any vegetation they attack, so they end up killing the plant because there's no more root system. They'll burrow under homes and damage foundations. They can uproot irrigation lines and sprinkler systems. They carry a wide assortment of diseases that can infect domesticated livestock as well as humans. They have no natural predators and are exceptionally adaptable to different climates and environments, so their population will continue to grow exponentially. Sows can produce litters averaging eight offspring every four or five months, and they can begin reproducing at six months of age. And to top it off, the more aggressive boars will attack pets and other small animals.

But guess what? Some of the animal rights people say the wild hog problem is exaggerated. They want hunters and state officials to leave the little darlings alone or, at most, neuter them to keep the population down. Killing wild hogs, said one Florida state official, is "barbaric and unnecessary."

From my perspective, any neutering that happens should be directed at know-it-all government bureaucrats who feel compelled to speak even when they know nothing – and I mean nothing – about the issue. However, my mom taught me never to speak ill of anyone, so I'll quote Porky Pig himself and say, "That's all folks!"

Chapter 12

Dragon Hunting

Talk about a blast from the past. Alligators are like modern-day dinosaurs. It's like having fire-breathing dragons – minus the fire breath – swimming in our waterways and crawling around our yards. They're beautiful in a scary-ugly way, and their very existence today is evidence of the critical importance of the U.S. Fish and Wildlife Service and the various state wildlife agencies.

Alligators have been hunted pretty hard in Florida for over two centuries. They were considered a "cash crop" and served as an important source of income for the early pioneer Floridians and for their Depression-era descendants. Through a combination of over-hunting and the loss of habitat due to the building boom of the 1950s and 60s, the gator population dropped off the proverbial cliff. Gators were classified as an endangered species in the mid-1960s. Strict enforcement by game wardens and the wildlife service agencies helped the gator population to rebound strongly and, by 1987, the species was removed from the endangered species list – sort of. Because gators look so much like their cousins – crocodiles and caimans – the Fish and Wildlife Service still considers them to be a threatened species and continues to regulate their harvest.

Whether threatened or not, alligators will continue to be a nuisance in Florida – partly because of their nature and partly because of the stupidity of their human neighbors. It's against the law for anyone in the state of Florida to harass or feed gators, but that doesn't stop it from happening. Lots of people down here have gators living in their backyards and they think it's kind of a cool novelty to hand-feed the animals. Once they start doing that the gator will lose its natural fear of humans and, even worse, will get hooked on a hassle-free source of food. That creates a very dangerous animal that will have to be destroyed by one of the state-regulated nuisance trappers.

Even when they're not being encouraged by easy food, gators often wander into residential neighborhoods and wind up in some of the darnedest places. A game warden friend told me about a woman who came home and heard something slithering around her house. She called the local wildlife officer and they found a four-foot gator that had crawled through the house's doggie door. One of the saddest stories I heard from my friend was about a little old lady who'd had her dog chained up in the back yard. She called to say someone had played a dirty trick on her and had taken her dog and replaced it with a gator who was now attached to the dog chain. When the warden arrived he had to tell the lady that her dog was still on the chain. One episode that happened in my neighborhood when I was a kid had to do with a lady who was walking her collie on a levy along the canal. A gator ran up out of the water, grabbed her dog and broke the leash. All she could do was scream and watch as the gator took her dog into the canal and disappeared under the water. There are a ton of heartbreaking stories like this because gators seem to really love dogs. I know of many instances where gators have climbed a chain link fence to get at a dog. That's probably hard for many people to believe, but the way I explain it is that gators have a great outboard and they've got four-wheel drive. There's pretty much nowhere a gator can't go if it wants to. And to make it worse, gators are extremely fast on land. They can't really run very far, but they could outrun a quarter horse at a short distance.

Gators are truly vicious animals, but the one thing you can say in their defense is that they don't kill just to kill. They kill to eat. They kill to survive. And when they're hungry they'll go after most anything. They're not scared off by the size of a potential prey by any means. They'll go after a big wild boar or a white tail deer. And if the opportunity is right, they'll attack a human also.

Gators will also go after smaller prey. One time I was bass fishing on a lake in Florida and found this little pocket that was covered with a dome of trees. It was nice and dark and looked like a perfect spot for bass. So I tossed a jig and almost immediately it was hit. It was a nice bass, maybe three pounds, and I was reeling him in when it jumped straight up about two feet out of the water. I love when bass do that, but this time it was not a pretty sight. A good-sized gator – about seven feet long – came out of nowhere and caught the bass in mid-air. I'd had gators chase top-water lures before and have accidentally snagged a couple, but I'd never seen never anything like this. The gator timed his attack perfectly and, because alligators are not the catch-and-release type, the bass was lost to me and all subsequent fishermen.

Because of their fierce nature and their proximity to urban and suburban areas, the gator population is closely monitored by the state and Federal wildlife agencies. Since 1987, Florida state biologists have taken a headcount of gators in all the different areas and released the appropriate number of hunting tags to thin down the herd. Hunting gators is a very dangerous activity, so it's highly restricted and heavily regulated. Hunters are not allowed to use hand guns or rifles because the wildlife agency doesn't want a gator to get shot – and perhaps only being wounded instead of killed – and then sinking and being lost. So the correct way to hunt gators has three steps. First you need to get a line attached to the gator using a crossbow, compound bow or harpoon. You can even use a fishing pole with a treble hook. The key thing is to ensure that you've got something in the gator's hide so you can keep track of where he is because the gator is going to dive and try to get away from you. Then you want to hit the gator with a strong grappling hook attached to a heavy rope.

The last step is the most dangerous. You need to pull the gator right up to the boat, and while you're doing that he's trying to bite anything and everything. Gators will bite the side of the boat and they are unbelievably strong. They're going to pull the boat all over the place; and you've got to be very careful to keep your feet and hands away from the ropes because gators will snatch them if given half a chance. If you get a line wrapped around your arm or ankle, you'll get knocked overboard and the gator will have something more to snap at that the side of the boat. During my most recent gator hunt in the summer of 2011, my friend, Jerry, almost lost the tip of his finger. The gator pulled the line and in an instant it was wrapped around his finger and digging in tight. If I hadn't had my pocketknife and chopped the line real fast, he would have lost his finger. In addition to snapping its jaws, diving down and dragging the boat, the gator will also be twisting and spinning around. So when you're pulling the gator to the boat, you need to be patient, get everything lined up just right and wait for the perfect opportunity to hit him.

The deathblow is delivered with a .44 magnum bang stick that looks like a rifle barrel at the end of a six-foot pole. It fires on impact. You want to hit the gator right on the base of the neck where it meets the back of the skull. It's instant death for the animal, but he's still dangerous. That's because gators are reptiles and their slow metabolism and wacky nervous system allow their nerves and muscles to "react" for hours after they're considered physically dead. And while it would be painful to get bitten by any gator at any time – the pain would be nothing compared to the embarrassment of getting bit by a dead gator.

So this means that your job is not done when you've killed the gator with the bang stick. You now have to get his mouth taped shut – the same mouth that is snapping at you with its reptilian death rattles. You need two guys to do it safely. If it's a really big boy, you might even need a third. The trick is to get one hand on top of the gator's head and, being real careful not to get tangled up with his arms or legs that are still flailing around, you take your other hand, slip it around down by his shoulder, pull it up underneath the bottom jaw and push the two jaws together and hold them as tightly as you can. The other guy will run tape around the whole snout to keep it shut. I use electrical tape, but other guys use duct tape. It doesn't much matter – just make sure you use a lot of it.

The final step in the process is to put the tag on the gator immediately or once you get back to the boat ramp. Then, within 24 hours, you have to file a report either on paper or online to let the wildlife agency know that you filled that particular tag. You have to provide all the specifics about the catch -- the sex of the gator, its length, weight, and where you caught it.

I started hunting gators when I returned to Florida

from Ohio; and I find it an extremely challenging sport. Every hunt is a unique adventure. Gators are very stealthy. The best hunting time is at night so you've got to use spotlights to locate them and it's a real challenge to get up close. They're smart animals and they know when things aren't right. Nonetheless, I've been successful with my gator hunting and have been able to fill my tags every year. In the summer of 2011, Jerry and I had two tags and we filled both within the first week. We killed an eight-footer and a ten-footer. We passed up hundreds of gators to find these two mature animals who weren't just good-sized but would also make good eating. Alligator's a fine eating meat, but you have to pick your spots. A small gator won't have enough meat and a really big gator can be a little tough and harder to eat. I'd say that eight- to ten-footers are the prime eating gators. A ten-foot gator weighs about 450 pounds and provides 45 to 50 pounds of boneless prime cut meat – with the rest of the animal being bone, heavy skin, and a huge amount of guts. Some people will mount the heads, especially if it's a big bull gator, but the rest of the carcass is worthless. Some people think you can keep the skin and turn it into belts and boots, but it's a very expensive process to tan gator skin. Plus there's really no market for gator skins because of the huge commercial gator farms in Louisiana and other states.

The 400 or so pounds of leftover alligator carcass don't get wasted. We bring it to one of several bone yards in the Okeechobee area and within 24 hours there's nothing left. There are a lot of birds of prey down here, and the buzzards just clean house. But it's really the coyotes that do the majority of the feasting. One of the bone yards is on private land and we dug a pit to dump carcasses into. A lot of times we'll come back the next day and the carcass will have been dragged up and out of the pit by a pack of coyotes.

One of the funniest gator stories I've been part of happened a few years back. My good friend Bobby, who's since passed away, called to tell me he had a big gator on the line and needed some help bringing him in. I motored over there to help and immediately understood why he had called. This gator was absolutely gigantic – over 13 feet long and about 800 pounds. It took a while but we finally got the gator tied to the boat, and we pulled him through the locks and into the Clewiston channel. We got him as far as the boat ramp and realized that he was so big that there was no way we could lift him with the manpower we had. It was about 11 o'clock at night, and there was a local bar down the street. Bobby asked a friend to run over to the bar and find a couple of big, strong guys that could help us load the gator onto a truck bed. I was thinking in the back of my mind that this was going to be very interesting because the whole bar was going to show up and it was going to be a crazy scene. Sure enough, here comes car after car after car; people hootin' and hollerin' and they just surrounded the boat ramp. There were people standing everywhere and bunch of these heavy-duty drunk guys are blabbering about "Where's the gator?" and "Let's see this bad boy!" and "Bring him on." They're all standing real close to the water but the gator was totally submerged so no one could see him. We had a rope tied around the gator's neck and the rope was tied to the trailer hitch on my truck. I couldn't stop myself from making the most of the situation. I told the crowd to get ready and then I gave the truck a little extra gas. The gator flew out of the water like something from *Jurassic Park* and you wouldn't believe how fast a bunch of drunks could move. They were tripping and falling and trying their best to get the hell outta Dodge. No one could believe how big this gator was, and it was hilarious. I was sitting in my truck laughing so hard I couldn't see from the tears running down my face. After everyone calmed down and Bobby and I stopped laughing, we went to work trying to lift this guy into the truck. The best we could do was to get his head and shoulders in the back of my pickup truck with the tailgate down. We tied him down and I drove to the fish house with half the gator hanging out on the street, dragging the tail. The fish house lifted him with a forklift and weighed him in at 800 pounds. This gator's neck was as big as a 55-gallon drum. He was huge and scary, but I still laugh every time I think about that night.

That was my funniest encounter with a gator. My scariest encounter happened when I was a boy of twelve or thirteen. My buddy, Rob, and I were exploring the old St. Lucie River in a 10-foot Jon boat. This one stretch of the river had big palm trees that grew out of the bank and over the top of the water. We always used to run the boat right up underneath the trees to get to our favorite fishing spots. One day we were coming around a corner with me sitting in front and Rob in back handling the outboard. There was a huge palm tree hanging over the water and we spotted four legs hanging down. I looked up and saw a gator that was every bit of 12 feet and 600 pounds. Its gut was hanging down on each side of the branch like big saddlebags. It's not uncommon to see gators in trees. They'll often climb up and lie on a branch to soak up some sun. Well this particular gator was sunning itself no more than six feet over my head. I ducked down with my hands covering my head because I knew what was going to happen. Rob couldn't slow the boat because it would have stopped right underneath the tree. So he gave it full throttle and also ducked. Rob saw the gator jump off the tree and fall through the air. The gator barely missed us, hit the outboard, and landed in the water. I turned around to look at Rob and saw that he was as pale as I felt. We both just about crapped our pants, realizing that we were just a fraction of a second away from getting crushed to death. The funny thing is that the gator was probably just as scared as us. He wasn't attacking us; he was trying to get away from us. Whenever gators get spooked or feel that something isn't quite right, they get in the water. It's their security blanket, where they feel safest, most confident, and most powerful.

I'm so happy that these prehistoric-looking creatures have made such a dramatic comeback. I'm happy for gators as a species and for me as someone who loves to watch them loll on the banks of Okeechobee. I also love the opportunity to hunt these magnificent animals and help maintain a stable and healthy population. Gators multiply quickly – not as fast as rabbits or hogs – but a mature female will lay 35 or so eggs in her nest, with about 15 emerging as live hatchlings. Even accounting for normal mortality rates and natural predators (plus the cannibalistic nature of adult gators), the gator population could easily double or triple in a single year. Without regulated hunting, gator numbers would quickly get too large for their habitat to handle and tragic encounters with people and our pets and livestock would become far more common. Nobody wants that. So working along with the wildlife agencies, hunters will continue to enjoy the hunting experience and experience the sweet taste of fresh gator meat. It's a win-win.

Chapter 13

A Special Place In My Heart

Of all the hunts I've been on, one remains darkest in my memory.

It was an afternoon hunt in Ohio with a good friend. It was snowy and cold, but a perfect day for hunting. The ground was wet so you could walk through the woods and not make a whole lot of noise. My friend and I were walking down a creek and we saw a deer in the distance. He was just standing quietly and didn't seem concerned about our presence. As we got closer we could see that something wasn't right with him. He was standing in the middle of the creek, which had iced over in parts, so we knew the water was freezing cold. The deer was bending down and dipping one of his front legs in the water. A few steps closer and I could tell that he was hurt real bad. He had clearly been hit by a car, and I could see that his leg was almost completely severed and hanging on by little more than skin. He must have been injured for a couple days or so because the almost-severed leg was very swollen. We then noticed that the hoof on his other front leg was totally torn off. The poor creature was just a mess, and we quickly realized that there was no way he was going to survive. We walked closer to him and he couldn't even move. He'd try to move and fall down. It was a heart-wrenching thing to see, and we had to quickly decide what to do.

I'm sure some people would suggest that we take him to a veterinarian. But that's not as easy, humane or sensible as it might sound. Sure, you can take domestic animals like dogs and cats to a vet, and you can have a vet come out and look at your horse or cow. But the idea that you could capture a deer or any other wild animal and bring it to a vet borders on the ridiculous. The shock you would put the animal through would likely kill it long before you reached the vet's office. In addition, there was no doubt in my mind that this deer could not be saved. He was badly injured, almost certainly had a lot of internal bleeding, probably hadn't eaten in several days, and couldn't move an inch in any direction. He was sick and in serious pain, and he was definitely going to die.

It was a horrible scene. I just felt so sorry for him, and in my mind there was only one thing to do. I couldn't just walk away and let him stand there and suffer. He might have lived another few days before he starved to death, bled out or got taken down by a predator. Like many people who spend a lot of time with nature – including hunters, farmers and ranchers – I've had to deal with a number of animals in this kind of situation. I knew the best thing to do – the most charitable thing to do – was to put him out of his misery. I was hunting with a compound bow, lined up the shot, and put him down. The poor thing was so weak that he was gone in a matter of seconds.

It was a mercy killing, done for all the right reasons, but it still brought me to the edge of tears. Life is the most precious thing in the universe. And whether it's a horse with a leg too shattered to repair or a beloved cancer-stricken dog, it's an emotional moment when you deliver the life-ending shot – whether from a needle, bow, or firearm. Anyone who loves animals must pause before administering that shot – not to weigh the pros and cons one final time, but rather to show respect for the life that was lived.

In addition to his external injuries, this particular deer had a major infection in his system and his meat was not fit for human consumption. So we dragged him out of the creek and placed him in the woods for predators to eat. It was a sin that the animal had to suffer, and it would have been another sin to have his meat go to waste. So we contributed to the circle of life and helped other animals to survive with nutrients from the deer's flesh. It was the best we could make out of a sad situation.

I encountered another sad situation a couple of years later. I was hunting in the woods and I noticed a young buck, what we call a knucklehead or a yearling buck. He came walking up right underneath my tree stand, so right away I knew something wasn't right with him. When I looked down I noticed that his hide was scuffed up and his upper jaw and nose were gone. I was pretty sure he'd been hit by a car and either run over or dragged for a distance. He couldn't eat or drink. What was remarkable, however, was that there wasn't a speck of blood on him. That's because deer are amazing animals that will work together and help protect each other. The other deer in his herd had licked him clean. But while he wasn't bleeding, he was slowly starving to death. There was no possible way this deer could survive. He hadn't been able to smell me and would never be able to smell a predator until it was too late. The poor thing was clearly confused. He didn't understand what had happened, where to go, or what to do. He was just shuffling around, touching what was left of his face to leaves and grass but unable to eat anything.

I was again faced with a painful choice. Should I let him walk off into the woods knowing he would starve or be attacked? I didn't know if he was in physical pain – though I assumed he had to have been – but he was clearly in shock and stressed out. I watched him for a while and made my decision. I had seen some other beautiful deer in the area and I had fully expected to harvest a champion specimen. I was holding one antlers deer tag and I chose to do the humane thing and use the tag on this poor creature. I was hunting with a muzzleloader, and I took a clean shot and he dropped immediately. When I climbed down from the tree stand I saw that he was beaten up worse than he had looked from a distance, but I was able to field dress him and keep some of the meat for venison hamburger and sausage. The rest was left for the scavengers of the forest.

Both of these animals had their lives cut short not by me, but by the cars and drivers that struck them down. It's something that happens every day across the country, but it needn't be that frequent. In all my years of traveling around the U.S. and touring as a professional bass fisherman, I've never hit a deer. And that's not because I'm such an exceptional driver. Rather it's because I pay attention. I understand that deer and other wildlife were here first, and they don't understand traffic lights, double lines, or caution signs. They just want to get from here to there; and to do that, they increasingly have to pass through or over man-made structures.

So please, if you remember just one thing from this book, have it be to slow down when you're driving, be careful and be on the lookout for wildlife. I love the fact that a lot of states are outlawing cell phone use while driving because it is very distracting, and when you're distracted you don't have the reflexes to avoid an accident. One of the most important things you can do when driving at night is to look for glowing eyes on the side of the road around woods, meadows, creek bottoms and other natural deer crossings.

There's a special place in my heart for these two deer that I had to put down. I fully understand that their lives don't even matter to most people, but they live forever in my memory. I hope the good Lord has a place up in heaven for all the wonderful creatures of the wild, and maybe I'll get a chance to meet these two deer and let them know that I cared then and I still care today.

Chapter 14

The Best Hunters of Them All

A few years ago, representatives from the Sierra Club and the U.S. Forest Service were meeting with Wyoming ranchers to discuss alternative approaches for controlling the coyote population. For as long as anyone could remember, the ranchers had used the tried-and-true method of shooting or trapping the predators. The Sierra Club proposed a more humane solution to the problem – capturing the animals alive. The males would then be castrated and released in the same area where they'd been caught. The ranchers thought about this idea for a couple of minutes. Finally an old fellow wearing a big cowboy hat in the back of the room stood up, tipped back his hat and said, "Gentlemen, I don't think you understand the problem. These coyotes ain't screwin' our sheep, they're eating them!"

This story has gone viral on the internet (and I'm kind of proud of the fact that I actually understand what that means). I can't vouch for the story's validity, but it does point out the disconnect that often occurs between ranchers and farmers who are trying to protect their livelihood and the various associations and governmental organizations that mean well but often seem to rely on theory and idealized visions of wildlife rather than the reality of the situation.

Wildlife predators are everywhere. And while I consider myself to be a pretty good hunter, my skills pale in comparison to coyotes, fox, wolves, bobcats and mountain lions. Those animals make their living by hunting, and they are responsible for killing five to ten times as many deer, elk, moose and caribou as my hunting brothers and I do in any given year. In the continental United States, fox are estimated to kill almost a million ducks per year; and during the Alaskan winter months, a single pack of wolves is estimated to kill a moose or deer every few days. And there are close to 2,000 wolf packs in the state.

Not that there's anything wrong with that. It's what predator animals do. They hunt to survive. The problem is that their appetite can extend far beyond their natural prey, especially when their numbers exceed what their territory can support. That's when predators – and coyotes in particular – start showing up in suburban and urban areas and start killing domestic animals and pets. My mom lost a cat to coyotes; and while attacks on children are rare, they do occur.

One thing that a lot of people don't know about coyotes, wolves or any feral canine is that they don't kill their prey before they eat it. Unlike bobcats or mountain lions, canines will literally rip the intestines out of an animal while it's still alive and leave the animal to die. Worst of all, they often kill just for the hell of it without eating their prey.

Another thing that few people realize is that predators tend to be lazy and, given the choice and the opportunity, they will attack the easiest target. That means a fenced-in dog, cat, sheep or goat is easier to catch than a scampering rabbit or whitetail. It was documented in Massachusetts that coyotes actually waited for people to leave their homes before attacking their pet dogs and cats. Guess that means coyotes are both lazy and smart.

When I first started hunting I knew very little about the ways of the woods and often didn't really understand what I was seeing or hearing. I recall one day in particular that opened my eyes to how much I needed to learn. It was a snowy morning in Ohio and I'd decided to go deer hunting with a compound bow. I got to my tree stand really early, about an hour before the sun rose. I find these early morning times very peaceful and relaxing, so I just about jumped out of my skin when I heard this loud noise that sounded just like a baby crying. It kept going on and then I heard a lot of commotion on the ground with branches breaking. At this point the hair was standing up on the back of my neck. All kinds of thoughts were running through my mind. Did someone lose or abandon their kid in the woods? I was too scared to get down from the tree to see what was going on. I might have felt differently if I'd had a gun, but all I had was a stick and a string. So I decided to just sit tight and wait for the sun to come up and see what I could find. Well the sun finally came up, and I spotted some deer and everything seemed peaceful and quiet. I didn't see any deer I wanted to harvest, so after a while I climbed down from the stand. I was still a little nervous about the ruckus I'd heard, but I also didn't want to tell anyone about it because they'd probably figure me for a fool – all scared of a couple of noises. I eventually felt compelled to find out what I had heard, so I described the sound to a couple of hunting buddies and they started laughing at me.

"Hah! You didn't know what that was, did ya?" they said.

I shook my head, and when they finally controlled their laughter enough to speak they told me that the bloodcurdling noise I'd heard was a rabbit. I figured they were kidding with me. How and why could a rabbit make that kind of noise? When I pushed the question, they told me that it was the sound a rabbit makes when it was being attacked by a coyote. The sound of being eaten alive.

Like most people I don't particularly like coyotes, but I also don't see any reason to confront them. Unfortunately that was the predicament I found myself in one day while deer hunting. I was up in my tree stand and I saw three coyotes come prancing along the tree line. They came right up to my tree and sat themselves down. I thought maybe I could shoot one of them, but I was shooting straight down and couldn't get a good line. So I decided to just sit there and watch what was going on. Well they made themselves comfortable and showed no sign of moving on. By this time the sun was going down fast and there was just a little bit of sunshine left; and then those suckers started howling. They kept it up for a good ten minutes, and it was killing my ears. It was like sticking your head up against a police siren. I finally got to the point where I couldn't take it anymore and I stood up in my stand and shouted, "Hey, that's enough of that." Well those three coyotes looked straight up at me and took off like a bat out of hell. I'd thought they were howling at me, but they were just communicating with their pack.

Predator populations in general and coyote populations specifically can easily get out of hand, and a lot of small game hunters and farmers love predator hunting. I'm not a predator hunter. I'll pop one every now and then but it's not something I want to hunt because I'm not going to eat it. I've had plenty of opportunity to shoot bear, for example, but I've never done it. Bear meat is very dark and reminds me of liver-and-onions. It's nothing I want to put in my mouth.

The guys who do actively hunt predators have my

wholehearted support. They're a necessity because farmers and ranchers often need someone to work their land for a few nights because the predators are killing their domestic farm animals, or their dogs and cats. Another reason I support predator hunting is that when they start getting too thick in an area, they'll often carry rabies and will pass it along to domestic animals.

Despite the nuisance factor, you always want to have predator animals around. They serve a purpose in keeping the various animal populations in balance. That's another reason why we all need to support our Fish and Game departments, wildlife biologists and wardens to find that balance. They're always watching. Right now, for example, they're closely watching the wolf program over in Yellowstone Park that is decimating the natural elk population.

That wolf reintroduction program in Yellowstone is a good example of misguided approaches to wildlife management. There's a vocal group of people who keep saying, "We want the wolves back. We want the wolves back." And they want to release the wolves in areas with huge cattle industries. Wolves are vicious animals by nature and right now they're killing almost all the baby elk being born in Yellowstone. They're also feasting on local free-range sheep and cattle. What I find interesting and disturbing about this issue is that the same people who advocate reintroducing wolves to cattle country would never suggest their release in Pennsylvania or upstate New York. No one's advocating that. This is one of those not-in-my-backyard issues. Everyone wants wolves to be free to roam – as long as they stay far away from children and pets. Wolf reintroduction people take on a whole different attitude when wolves show up in their own suburban neighborhoods. I guess it's okay for a rancher to lose 50 sheep to a single wolf (which actually happened in

1997 just outside of Yellowstone) as long as some New York investment banker doesn't have his prized pedigreed lapdog snatched away. In my view, both losses are terrible; but why do we open the door to the former? It doesn't make any sense. There are plenty of places where wolves currently exist and it works just fine. We don't need to be tampering with this just because some people think wolves should be free to roam wherever and whenever.

Now, I'm not usually a big fan of PETA, and I rarely agree with their teachings or philosophy. But when it comes to the reintroduction of predators, we're on the exact same page. This is a verbatim quote from the PETA.org website:

> *PETA does not support predator-reintroduction programs for myriad reasons. Animals can very often escape artificial boundaries and become a "nuisance," leading to their being poisoned, hit by cars, or shot. In failed attempts to escape, they might become entangled in barbed wire or be shocked by electric fences. Upon introduction to their new homes, their prey scatter, and their lives and behavior patterns are turned upside-down.*
>
> *Wolves, bears, lynxes, and boars deserve to lead free, natural lives. Reintroduction programs subject wild animals to capturing and handling, which is always very stressful for them and may eventually put them in the line of fire of farmers who are already angry about predator-reintroduction programs.*
>
> *To capture and transport wolves and other predators to a new area, the animals must first be tranquilized. When they recover from the*

anesthesia, they are released into unfamiliar terrain. This unnatural process causes a great deal of stress to animals and threatens their physical health and well-being.

Wolves are social animals who live in tightly knit packs. It is nearly impossible to capture and relocate an entire pack, so relocation almost always breaks up a tightly bonded extended family, likely causing loneliness, pining, separation anxiety, depression, and grieving.

Relocated animals often have difficulty determining where they can find food and shelter. Some of the wolves who were reintroduced into Yellowstone National Park have left their new packs because it is difficult to adapt to the new area and function in their contrived "family" units.

Reintroducing wolves and other predators into an environment that has been free of such animals for a long time is also traumatic for the animals who already live there, such as deer, birds, and any other animals who suddenly find themselves being stalked and attacked.

While supporters of predator-reintroduction programs believe in the concept of restoring the "balance of nature," it's not possible to artificially impose this balance. Ecosystems are in a constant state of change, which has been sped up by human expansion and technological advances.

Our species has wiped out predator populations in many areas of the world but must also realize that the system has evolved and *recovered to its current state.*

Rather than attempting to return wilderness areas to some semblance of an undefined previous state and manipulating populations of animals, we need to focus our efforts on alleviating the suffering and promoting the well-being of those who are there now.

Many articles and news reports about the wolf-reintroduction program in the U.S. focus on people's interests—the idea that the absence of wolves makes us miss out on a majestic part of nature. Such reports romanticize hearing "the cry of wolves" one day again in Yellowstone but do not consider the extensive suffering that could be expressed in these cries.

I couldn't have said it better myself.

Chapter 15

Guns, Germs, Fangs and Starvation

There's a great scene in *My Cousin Vinny*, a very funny movie about a New York lawyer trying a case in Alabama. Vinny is telling his girlfriend, Mona Lisa, that he's going deer hunting with the opposing lawyer. Vinny is wondering what pants to wear and asks for Mona Lisa's opinion. This was her response:

> *Imagine you're a deer. You're prancing along. You get thirsty. You spot a little brook. You put your little deer lips down to the cool clear water...bam! A freakin' bullet rips off part of your head! Your brains are laying on the ground in little bloody pieces! Now, I ask ya, would you give a crap what kind of pants the son-of-a-bitch who shot you was wearing?!*

Mona Lisa shares the attitude of many Americans that hunting is a cruel and horrible way for deer and other wild creatures to die. I would argue that, given the alternatives, hunting is one of the most humane things we can do for the wildlife that we share God's earth with. I have strong opinions about this topic, but I'm just a redneck high school dropout whose opinion wouldn't count for much to most people. But the good news is that this redneck high school dropout has a lot of smart friends and I've asked them to contribute their thoughts.

Larry Martgolio

Larry is a wildlife biologist who has done a lot of research on the fluctuations of deer population. He points to a study in Illinois that concluded an annual harvest of 34% of the deer population was necessary to keep it stable.

Once the dynamics of deer populations had been studied, it turned out that the proportion of does over the age of two-and-a-half was the major factor in growth or decline. Older does have more twins so this increases the fawns-to-does ratio. A simple example, assuming annual mortality remains constant, is a population of 100 deer in an area comprising 25 bucks, 34 adult does and, with a ratio of 1.2 fawns per doe, 41 fawns (21 of which would be buck fawns). The next year, adding the female fawns to the doe population, there would be 46 bucks, 54 does, and again at 1.2 fawns per doe, 63 fawns, for a new total of 163 deer. After another year, the population would be doubled or more. Keep in mind that one buck can breed with multiple does, so bucks-only hunting does not control a population. Only harvesting a substantial number of adult does, lowering the fawn-to doe ratio, will accomplish that. Studies have shown it is impossible to harvest all the antlered bucks in legal season, so there are always enough left to keep the does breeding.

As a wildlife biologist in Wisconsin in the 1970s, I witnessed how hard it is, even for very adaptable deer, to have a stable population in the face of severe winter weather. The winters of 1975 through 1977 were some of the worst on record. The deer slowly starved to death and, after those three bad winters, deer populations were estimated to be less than 5 per square mile where, under normal conditions, there might be 80 to 120 deer per square mile.

Tom Meredith

Tom is a Wyoming-based rancher and hunting guide, and he agrees with Larry about the need to control deer populations for humane reasons.

I had a neighbor in Wyoming who owned 3200 acres but was against hunting. I once sat on a county road with the chief enforcement officer for Wyoming Game and Fish, looking at 65 acres of this man's irrigated hay ground. By four o'clock in the afternoon we had counted 472 whitetail. The officer went to the landowner and told them he really should allow some hunting or disease and starvation would wipe out most of the deer. The officer explained that there were hundreds of locals who would love to have that meat in their freezers to feed their families through the winter. Indeed, to many of those families that meat meant the difference between eating or going hungry. The landowner let a few hunters in, but they only harvested about 40 deer. Later that winter on a cold January day, I drove out that same county road heading into town. I saw a group of five deer huddled close together in a foot of snow. I drove back home about two hours later and saw the same five deer in the exact same spot all dead from starvation. That is incredible cruelty. How could anyone prefer deer to suffer starvation and slow death rather than a quick harvest and complete use and enjoyment of the meat?

I have driven through ranches with so many dead deer and antelope that even the scavengers couldn't keep up. Buzzards, magpies, eagles, fox, coyote, skunk, and raccoon all feasted but dozens of deer and antelope lay untouched. They're usually scattered across the hills and clustered around the water holes. I once came across the skeletons of 50 or 60 antelope after a particularly cold and snowy winter. They were clustered together in a small valley and had starved to death because there was nothing left to eat. The prior year we had been hunting that area and saw herds of 250 and 300 -- far too many for that part of Wyoming. It is so very sad, and one of the things that proper game management can help to prevent.

Starvation is just one of the issues that afflict deer when their population exceeds what the land can support. Diseases also run rampant.

Tom Meredith

Disease does proliferate during times of deer overpopulation, and one of the worst is called Blue Tongue. It is seen most often in times of overpopulation and drought. Too many animals at the same water source, and the virus spreads like wildfire. Domestic livestock can be vaccinated for it, but it can affect all ruminants. The animal's tongue starts to swell, and they begin to suffocate. I have watched deer and antelope slamming their heads into the ground trying to get air. Once this starts it can be a matter of only a couple hours before they die. As a humane person, I wish I could put them out of their misery. As a legal hunter, I can't.

In addition to the diseases that deer suffer as a result of overpopulation, deer are also responsible for the huge increase in Lyme disease in the northeastern part of the United States. Lyme disease is transmitted via deer ticks. The southern version of Lyme disease is STARI – or Southern-Tick Associated Rash Illness – and is spread by lone star ticks.

Larry Martgolio

While the reasons are not fully understood, the lone star tick shows up far more frequently in areas with deer overpopulation. The lone star tick uses deer mice, a common mammal, as an alternate host and quickly spreads to most warm-blooded mammals, including humans. Lone star ticks lay their eggs on low vegetation, and the resulting swarms of juveniles wait for some passing animal they can attach to and begin developing into adults. As an example both the Mogan Ridge area of Indiana's Hoosier National Forest and the Beaver Creek Wilderness area in Kentucky's Daniel Boone National Forest were utilized to build deer populations to high levels for restocking in other areas of the states. Outdoor activities during the warm months are almost unbearable because of the prevalence of ticks in those areas. Lone star ticks, however, are not found anywhere else in the two states.

And then we come to predators. Many good-intentioned but misinformed people suggest that the deer population is exploding because of a lack of natural predators. (I won't even argue the point that man has been a natural predator of deer since the very first deer walked on the earth.) Some of these people go so far as to suggest the reintroduction of natural predators like wolves and mountain lions. I'll let my buddy Tom explain the lunacy of this approach.

Tom Meredith

Some say that predation should be the controlling factor instead of hunting. Then when these natural predators are found in their backyards, fish and wildlife officers are called in to kill them. Man is a predator and is a natural part of the food chain. There is no going back. The true hunter loves wildlife more than any other person on earth. He has seen the tragedy of starvation and disease; and he knows that working with Game and Fish departments across the country, he can make a positive difference in the survival of all natural species.

Introducing predators is not the answer. In an article in the "West Yellowstone News," the author states, "The annual aerial survey of the herd conducted during December 2010 resulted in a count of 4,635 elk, down 24% from the previous year. There has been about a 70% drop in the size of the northern elk herd since 1995 and the start of the wolf restoration program in Yellowstone National Park." Some people think this is a step in the right direction. But what happens when the wolves run out of elk to kill? They'll move out of the park and start to prey on livestock.

And by the way, those people who promote the "majestic wolf" should watch them make a kill sometime. Wolves eat the animal alive. Alive. Most victims die of shock as they are disemboweled. And wolves do not eat all that they kill. They often kill and then move on to kill again – leaving the disemboweled dying animals to suffer. Wolves don't return to their victims; they are just practicing and having fun.

Yellowstone is not an island onto itself. It is part of a greater ecosystem that includes humans and their livestock. Since the wolf introduction, the Wyoming economy has taken a huge blow. The Game and Fish department has rightly lowered the number of hunting licenses available because there are fewer animals to hunt. The repercussions of this have been devastating. Ranchers and outfitters, hotels and restaurants, gas stations and grocers, and every small town in Wyoming and Montana that used to base their livelihood on the hunting season now often rely on food stamps to put food on their family's table. And for what? So a few housewives in Maryland or New York can feel good at night knowing they saved the wolf – an animal that was doing quite well on its own and never needed saving in the first place.

I'll close this chapter on the benefits of hunting versus death by disease, starvation or fanged predators by quoting from "Wanted: More Hunters," an Audubon Society article published in March 2002:

America's deer crisis isn't confined to human population centers. In all 50 states it extends to wildland (sometimes vast tracts) where deer – including elk, moose, caribou, blacktails, whitetails, mule deer, and such aliens as axis deer – are managed more by superstition than science. First we killed too many whitetails, then too few. They've increased from an estimated 500,000 in 1900 to an estimated 33 million today, and they now occur in all 48 contiguous states. There is even concern that the explosion will cause the extinction of mule deer because whitetail bucks will breed with mule deer does, producing sterile males.

No state had managed its deer more abominably than Pennsylvania, but now it's leading the way. Backed by the Pennsylvania Habitat Alliance – a coalition of conservation, sportsmen's, and land trust groups put together by Pennsylvania Audubon and its partners – the state game commission is allowing and urging hunters to shoot more deer, especially does. If the herd is reduced to carrying capacity, deer will be bigger and healthier. Ruined range that can't support deer now will be able to do so, and there will be far more habitat for other wildlife, including other game species. "The commission has finally seen the light," comments Pennsylvania Audubon's director, Cindy Dunn. "This is precedent-setting. We think Pennsylvania can become a national model, where the hunter's role changes from resource taker to provider of an environmental and ecological service."

Please take a moment to re-read that last sentence, because that's my personal dream – to have everyone recognize the fact that hunters are environmentalists and ecologists who love wildlife, love nature, and would never do anything to jeopardize the quality of life of any living creature. Never.

Chapter 16

Smoke Poles

I don't know about you, but I've always loved driving cars and trucks with a manual transmission. The whole process of timing your shift, pressing down and easing up on the clutch pedal, listening to the engine, and feeling the gears engage is a lot of fun. It gets you much more involved in the mechanics of the car and the feel of the road than with an automatic transmission. Now I fully admit that when I'm towing my 20-foot bass boat, I'm mighty glad that my truck is an automatic. But for times when you're just tooling around the countryside, nothing beats a stick shift.

I feel the same way about guns, and that's why I'm a big fan of muzzleloaders.

By now you probably have the distinct feeling that I'm a traditionalist. Maybe you even think that I'm an old-fashioned son of a gun. And I guess I am. But I'm proud of it. I love reading about the history of our country and visiting the sites of historic battles and major events. Part of me wishes I had been born in an earlier time, and muzzleloading guns provide me an opportunity to experience a little bit of what life was like for our ancestors.

But it wasn't a love of history that first got me involved with muzzleloaders; it was a love of hunting and the outdoors. When I arrived in Ohio, I landed a shift job with odd hours. I'd work for seven days and get five days off. Then I'd work another seven days and get four days off. That meant I had a lot of time on my hands and I spent almost all of it in the woods. I would literally spend from sunrise to sundown outside. And as I got more and more interested in hunting, I realized that I was missing out on a whole hunting season. I was hunting during bow season and gun season, but I was shut down during muzzleloading season. That meant I was sitting in the house with nothing to do, so I had to get involved with black powder.

Like most everything else in my life, I started from the ground up with muzzleloading. I went to a local gun shop, got some advice from the owner, and bought a kit from the Traditions Firearms Company. I'd been around guns my entire life, but building my own gun was a whole different ballgame. I was real excited when I opened the box, saw all the parts and started reading the instructions. I quickly got hooked, and you will too if you give it a try. The cool thing about muzzleloading kits is the variety. Muzzleloaders are like an art form onto themselves. You can get traditional hunting rifles, Revolutionary War style long rifles that are almost five-feet in length, pistols, revolvers, and even miniature cannons – and you usually have a choice between flintlock and percussion models. And because everything in the kit is in the rough, you really get to customize the gun so it's unique to you. You need to sand and finish the wooden stock with stain and varnish. Most kits offer a variety of woods and brass inlays. The barrel and other metal pieces all come as raw steel. You don't need to sand them but you do have to blue the metal yourself. The metal pieces come coated with a thin layer of grease so they won't rust in the package. You need to clean all the metal with alcohol and then rub it down with a bluing solvent so it turns the blue-gray gunmetal color that we're all familiar with. The bluing process is not just for cosmetics; it also serves to strengthen the metal and prevent rust. The whole process is a lot of work, but it's well worth it. You'll have made something that is uniquely yours and that will provide years of enjoyment.

Muzzleloading is not for everyone. Even if you skip the kit-making and buy a ready-made gun, you still have a lot of work in front of you. When it comes to working with black powder, cleanliness is next to godliness. And there's a lot of cleaning involved with black powder. A real lot. You have to clean the gun every couple of times you shoot it. It's not a terribly complicated process and most people get the hang of it after a few times; but it definitely is time-consuming and, if it's not a labor of love, it will probably drive you crazy and turn you away from black powder weapons.

But if you grow to love muzzleloaders like I have, you can enjoy the sport in a wide variety of ways. Some guys like to go all out and outfit themselves with buckskin and raccoon hats and do it just like the pioneers with the old flintlock. There are also a lot of guys like me who love the black powder experience but who modify the guns so they're easier for cleaning. Whichever approach you take, black powder hunting is a very traditional sport that gets you more involved in and focused on the whole process.

Think about it this way. You've hand-loaded a round and you know you've only got one shot, so you're going to make sure that bullet counts. You're not going to go out and take any slop shot that you can. Black powder makes the hunter think about everything he does. It keeps him dialed in and focused. Black powder hunters will pass on smaller animals and wait for bigger and better opportunities – and make sure they have a really good shot because with muzzleloaders it's one and done.

Technically, of course, you can reload a muzzleloader in the field but it's a slow and difficult process. I usually carry a speed loader that already has the measured powder and the bullet so I can reload pretty darn fast. But even if I go as fast as I possibly can, you're still talking at least a full minute before it's ready to go again. And that's the good news. The bad news is that by the time you reload pretty much every critter within hearing and seeing distance has boogied far far away.

The reloading time isn't the only issue with firing a muzzleloader. We call black powder guns "smoke poles" because when you fire them they let out a big cloud of smoke. That means you have to wait for the fog to clear to see what happened. Unlike with a traditional rifle or bow, you can't tell if your shot hit the animal or missed him by a mile. The smoke cloud also drifts through the woods and will spook any animal who hasn't already been frightened off by the sound of gunfire. So like I said, when you hunt with a muzzleloader you have to make every shot count – and that means a lot of time on the practice range.

It also means you have to practice with the same gun and the same ammunition you plan to hunt with. Each make and model of muzzleloader shoots a little differently and favors a specific type of ammunition so you have to play around to find the best combination. That's part of the fun and a big part of the challenge of the sport. I had an 1800s-style Traditions percussion-cap gun and I experimented with a variety of bullets but I couldn't get it dialed in. It would shoot all over the place. So I got to thinking that I should try a traditional round ball – which is exactly what it sounds like: a round ball bullet that looks like a lead marble. You wrap the ball in a piece of cloth lubricated with bore butter and push it down the barrel. Well that round ball put the magic back in the gun. It was dead on. I mean you could have driven a nail with that combination of gun and bullet it was so accurate.

Trial and error is the key to success with muzzle-loaders, especially when built from a kit. So when you buy your gun, you should buy a pack or two of several types of bullets. (I say "bullet" but you're not buying bullets with powder, you're just buying the tips – also known as slugs.) There are all kinds of different slugs for muzzleloaders. I shoot a 50-caliber Thompson Center muzzleloader but what I'm actually shooting is a 44-magnum hollow point bullet wrapped in a plastic sleeve called a sabot. It's a lighter bullet that lets me pick up more speed, shoot a little flatter, and extend my range.

You test the accuracy of your gun and ammo combination by target shooting in sets of three. You aim for the center of the target; but if your first bullet hits to the left of the target, you don't try to adjust. You aim at the center again, see where it hits, and then shoot again aiming at the center. If all three bullets align on the target within a quarter's diameter of each other, then you've got a pattern going. That's when you align your sights to adjust for the off-target trail of the bullet. If you shoot three bullets and one is off-target to the left, one's off to the right and one's down low then – assuming that you're an accurate shot and it's not a case of user error – you know the bullet is not right for that gun. So the point is that you need to play around with different ammo combinations, and when you find the winner you just know it. It feels right and it shoots right.

And I guess that's the biggest reason to try your hand at muzzleloading. It feels right.

We live in a world of unbelievable technologies. The stuff that I read about in science fiction stories when I was a kid is now real. And I can't complain about it. I have a smartphone and a computer. I use email and I love losing myself in a football game on my high-definition television. But I also love the simple things in life. Frying a couple of eggs in a cast iron pan. Watching dolphins romp around and play with each other in the ocean. Casting a rubber worm at daybreak. And perhaps most of all, the elegant simplicity of loading and shooting a black powder rifle and revisiting the lives and times of our forefathers.

Try it. You'll like it.

Chapter 17

A Stick and A String

It's been said that the quickest way to a man's heart is through his stomach, and that sure speaks to how I got interested in archery.

It happened back in the early 1980s, when I was working in the commercial fishing industry. One of the guys my brother and I worked for had a house way out in the country. We used to do a lot of the net work out there in the off-season – inspecting and repairing the nets and getting everything ready for the next fishing season. One morning we arrived at his house and he was nowhere to be found. We figured he had gone out on an errand or something, so we started working. A few hours later, he drove up in his truck and waved at us with a big smile. He hopped out of the cab carrying a compound bow and wearing full camouflage gear. He asked us to give him a hand and, together, we pulled a big buck out of the truck bed. My brother and I watched in amazement as he butchered and cleaned the animal. He had clearly done this many times and he worked quickly and efficiently, harvesting every edible piece of meat. It was getting near lunchtime so he took some of the venison into the house, rolled it in breadcrumbs and pan-fried it. Well I'd eaten a lot of good food in my life – ranging from the lobster meat my grandmother used to cook for breakfast to freshly caught catfish and snapper – but nothing I'd ever tasted was as delicious, tender and full of flavor as my first taste of venison. I learned later that this deer had been feeding in a nearby orange grove, eating the oranges as well as the leaves, and that contributed mightily to its flavor.

Chris and I were chowing down like we hadn't eaten in a month, and all the time we were looking at each other, nodding and thinking the exact same thing: "We gotta get us some of this stuff." We had done some hunting prior to this, and I had shot a deer a few months earlier (though a friend took the deer home and I never got to taste it); but this meal really whetted our appetite for a steady diet of venison. Chris and I were always looking for good adventures, and we knew that archery was something we could have a lot of fun with.

I actually got my first bow and arrow set as a Christmas present when I was five or six years old. Chris and I spent many happy hours practicing in the back yard, shooting at trees and bullseye targets, and having mock tournaments against each other. We got to be pretty good shots, but we never hunted with bows and our focus when we were young was fishing.

That all changed after we tasted fresh venison. Chris and I started shopping around that very afternoon, hoping to buy a couple of nice – but not too expensive – bow and arrow sets. We found a local archery store and the shopkeeper gave us a decent deal on two compound bow outfits. He taught us a bit but the reality was that we were rank amateurs. There was no one around to teach us so we pretty much just learned on our own. We practiced every chance we could, and the following season we got our licenses and began to hunt on public land. In truth, we called it hunting but it was more like sightseeing and hiking in the woods. Chris and I are both big guys so we probably sounded like a pair of Sasquatches tromping around. I mean we were absolutely no threat to any living creature. We saw a lot of animals but never got close enough to even get a shot off. That's the bad news. But the good news is that we always had a great time; and that's one of the lessons I always try to share with people. You don't have to kill an animal to have a great hunt and a wonderful time.

Since that first unsuccessful season, I've become a pretty good archer with a lot of confidence in my ability and my equipment. I've also seen the sport change dramatically over the years. When I first took up archery, most everyone was shooting and hunting with traditional long bows. The basic design of the equipment went back over 20,000 years and was tried-and-true. Think about it. Up until the invention of gunpowder and firearms, the bow and arrow was the weapon of choice in both hunting and warfare. And you could make a pretty strong argument that the invention of the bow and arrow was one of the most important milestones in human history – turning our ancestors into proficient hunters who could now have a steady supply of nourishing protein.

Just as high-tech composite materials have trans-formed golf and competitive cycling, the world of archery has also benefitted from the use of lighter and stronger materials like graphite. Arrows can be lighter and, as a result, faster. The bow's limbs can be manufactured to tighter tolerances and deliver more consistent results. And just like in golf, these improvements allow more people to enjoy the sport and perform at a higher level. And that's good.

The most significant innovation in archery arrived in 1966 in the form of the compound bow. In just forty-five years it's become the most popular bow in the United States and is far and away the bow of choice for hunters. Without getting into the nitty gritty details, a compound bow basically uses leverage – provided by a series of cables and pulleys – to bend the limbs. This creates a very efficient exchange of energy that makes compound bows much easier to use by smaller and less strong archers. It's especially valuable for people with disabilities. The other benefit of compound bows is that they are shorter than traditional bows and much easier to carry and shoot from blinds and tree stands.

The biggest advantage of compound bows – beyond their increased efficiency and smaller size – is their accuracy. In strictly technical terms, compound bows are not more accurate than traditional bows; but they are certainly much easier to shoot accurately. It's similar to the situation with modern golf clubs – they're much more forgiving. For the new or less experienced archer or hunter, you'll be much less likely to make a mistake with a compound bow. And from a hunting standpoint, that means fewer missed shots and a more humane kill.

The increased accuracy comes from the fact that compound bows have actual sights on them while traditional long bows use instinctive sighting. Once you have your compound bow fitted and adjusted, you'll have pins for different distances. On my bow, for example, I have my first pin set at 10 and 20 yards. So if I'm shooting at a target 10 to 20 yards away, that's the pin I'm going to focus on. And then I have 30-, 40- and 50-yard pins. I don't recommend that anyone, no matter how good, try and shoot an animal from more than 30 yards with an arrow. Ideally you want to be inside of 20 yards for two reasons. First, accuracy and striking power fall off with increased distance. Secondly, many animals – especially whitetail – will jump when they hear the snap of a string. They can move awfully fast and even the best-aimed shot can miss badly.

There's another type of bow that's popular with target shooters and hunters. It's the crossbow and it's been around since the fourth century. The basic design consists of a bow that's mounted horizontally on a wooden or metal stock. The string is pulled back and held in place until released by a trigger-like mechanism. Regulations on the use of crossbows for hunting vary state by state. Some states don't allow crossbows at all, while others only allow them for people with physical handicaps. Some states have separate crossbow and traditional archery seasons, and some combine the two into a single season.

Many people have the mistaken belief that crossbows are frowned upon because they are more deadly, but that's not really the case. I think it's more a case of some outdated laws. When crossbows first became popular, traditional bow hunters complained that they weren't fair. Traditionalists argued that crossbow hunters were cheating because they didn't have to draw down on the deer. Part of the trick of bow hunting is that you've got this animal within 10 or 20 yards of you and, with a long bow or compound bow, you have to draw back without scaring the animal. You avoid that step with a crossbow and eliminate any body motion. You just raise the crossbow, get the pin on the animal, and let it fly.

The biggest advantage of crossbows is their speed. They shoot a lighter arrow – usually called a bolt – and they shoot fast. As a point of comparison, when I was a young buck I used to shoot 70- and 80-pound bows. Now, as I'm getting older, I tend to shoot a 60-pounder and I'll offset that with lighter arrows to keep up my speed. But I won't get the penetration that an archer shooting a heavy bow with a heavy arrow and heavy tip would. At 60 pounds, I'm still shooting a really good hunting bow; but even the small crossbows have a

150-pound draw and hit with a lot of authority. The best crossbows are shooting at speeds up to 300 feet per second.

I always tell people that there are a ton of variables in archery, and you need to choose the equipment that best suits you and your intended usage. For example, I still prefer compound bows for hunting. I own a crossbow and have done a lot of target practice shooting with it, but I've never taken it to the woods. I have used a crossbow for gator hunting but that's it. I have a lot of confidence in my compound bow, probably because that's what I grew up with and what I've spent the most time with. I also use a traditional longbow once in a while – but only for bow fishing, not for deer or other game.

In addition to the type of bow, hunters have to understand the various types of arrowheads and choose the head that's right for the game. It took me a lot of experimentation and study to determine that mechanical broadhead tips are my choice for hunting whitetail. They penetrate well and leave a good exit wound for an easy-to-follow trail and a quick kill. On the other hand, when it comes to hunting hogs with their thick leathery hide, I find that razor tips do a much better job. Razor tips will go right through the animal like a warm knife through butter, and the hog will fall a lot faster.

Archery is kind of like riding a bike in that, once you get the hang of it you're set for life. But it's also like playing the piano or some other musical instrument; you have to practice like crazy to keep your skills up. The difference is that if you get out of practice and make a mistake while playing the piano, no real harm is done. However, if you make a mistake with a hunting bow, you could seriously injure an animal without killing it. And in my mind that's not ethical. As I've said repeatedly in this book, hunting is a humane activity. But you have to be good at it. And to stay good you have to practice – and practice all year long, not just during hunting season.

One of the most important things I learned when I first began bow hunting is that there was a huge difference between target shooting and hunting. The target hunting environment tends to be very stable with flat and firm standing surfaces, unobstructed views of the target, and none of the urgency that tenses your muscles, gets the adrenaline flowing, and coats your hands and fingers with a film of nervous sweat. When hunting in the field, conditions change every second. Your stance might be crouching or kneeling. Depending on the terrain, you might be standing with one foot higher than the other or have to straddle a rock formation or fallen branch. You might be sitting in a tree stand and shooting downward. Weather conditions – including wind speed and direction, humidity, and visibility – also have a big impact when hunting. None of this can truly be replicated when target shooting; but if you keep these differences in mind as you practice with your bow, you'll be able to reap the maximum benefit from the practice sessions and optimize your hunting experience.

I consider myself an above-average archer and I've won several tournaments at local clubs, but I'm definitely not ready for prime time. That fact came through loud and clear when I attended a combined college and professional tournament at Miami University in Oxford, Ohio. I was totally blown away by what these young, old, and middle-aged folks were able to do with a stick and a string. Their skill levels made the splitting of an apple by William Tell seem like child's play. If you ever get a chance to attend a tournament in your area, jump at it. You'll be just as astounded as I was.

And if your only experience with archery was shooting a bow at a summer camp when you were in grammar school, visit your local archery club, talk to some archery enthusiasts and find out what you've been missing.

Chapter 18

The Family That Hunts Together

When you really think about it, our day-to-day lives are all about routine. You get up, go to work, come home, and go to bed. You do that hundreds of times a year; and if somebody asked you to remember a specific day at work, you'd probably come up blank because they're all pretty much the same. But when you take a child, sister, nephew, or spouse fishing, mushroom hunting, deer hunting, hiking, or just splashing around in a creek, you're creating a memory that lasts a lifetime. Every single hunting trip with a friend or loved one is etched into my heart. Taking my daughter to a fishing tournament or into the woods to see the wild hogs and watching her eyes light up are experiences that I will take to my grave. And anyone who doesn't take the time to create those kinds of experiences and memories is missing out on something very, very special.

Some of my fondest memories revolve around hunting experiences with my wife, K.C. Unlike me, K.C. did not grow up around hunting. She was kind of a city girl from Ft. Lauderdale. She was open-minded about hunting but she didn't really know what to expect. She knew I liked to hunt a lot and decided she wanted to give it a try. Turns out she loved the experience of being outdoors all day. We have a nice little hunting camp in central Georgia and K.C. loves being there. She likes the fact that there's no cell phone service. She can get up in the morning, sit on the porch, curl up with the dogs in a big blanket, read a book and listen to the quiet.

To this day, K.C. doesn't like to get up early to do a morning hunt; but when evening time comes, she de-scents, puts on her camo, and is ready to go. She almost never misses an evening hunt. I love to watch her intensity as she tries to spot an animal. It's fun and it keeps us close.

One of the very first times I took K.C. hunting, we were sitting in a homemade tower stand made out of plywood. There was absolutely nothing going on, but we were enjoying watching the birds and the other small critters going about their business. We hadn't seen a single deer and it was getting pretty dark, so we decided to climb down. K.C. – who's ever the optimist – said we should move real slow and be really quiet because we still might see a deer. Well, at this point, I'd been holding in a fart for well over an hour. I mean this thing was fully charged and ready for launch. As we began to climb down from the tower stand, I tried to squeak out a quiet one to relieve the pressure; but the thing ripped out of me like a turbocharged Formula 1 race car. I froze and looked at K.C. She started laughing so hard she was choking and that made me laugh, and that was a fitting end to our hunt day.

The next few times K.C. and I went hunting together, we tried a ground blind and a couple of tree stands. When we finally saw a deer, we just stayed motionless and watched it. I'd already decided in my mind that I wouldn't shoot the first deer that we saw even if it was a monster. I wanted to see K.C.'s reaction and it was everything I expected and more.

Her eyes just lit up with amazement and joy as she saw how close the deer would come to us. It was a very special moment that perfectly set the stage for one of the funniest moments I've ever experienced.

It happened during that first season of K.C. and I hunting together. I had taken her to a two-man ladder stand set up in a patch of real shady and thick hardwood trees. We climbed up in the ladder and, other than some pigs off in the distance, everything was quiet. All of a sudden I saw a small doe walking straight towards us. I looked at it and didn't see an ounce of fear in its eye. I didn't even think about pulling the trigger on such a young doe, and so she walked right up to our ladder stand till she was standing directly underneath us. The ladder stand was not very tall but it did have a good amount of camouflage meshing around it. K.C. started to lean over the rail to look down at the deer and she looked like she was in heaven. She was totally delighted and amazed by the experience. The deer was chewing on some leaves, picking up acorns and acting calm as could be. Then the doe scraped a stick with its leg and scared itself half to death. That crazy doe jumped straight up in the air and just about kissed K.C. right on the nose. The doe came down on its front legs and all K.C. could see was this big white butt straight up in the air beside her. The deer landed on the ground, spun in a complete circle, and looked around. When she saw that there was nothing to fear, she just went back to grazing. K.C. and I got the biggest thrill from seeing that deer jump up like that and it's a story we love to tell and re-tell.

Another of our favorite hunting stories involves a scarier experience. K.C. and I were in a tree stand deep in the woods and the sun was going down fast. All of sudden we heard a ferocious growl. I like to say it sounded like Barry White gargling peanut butter. Anyway, we heard this really deep growl that went on and on; and you could tell it was coming out of some really big lungs. I knew it was a couple of big boars trying to intimidate each other and getting ready to fight. They were really close to us and we could hear other hogs crashing through the underbrush, squeaking and squawking as they tried to get out of the way. Well K.C. was certifiably terrified. She kept saying how dark it was and asking how we'd ever get out of there. I tried my best to calm her down and told her that we were probably going to see a couple of hogs beating on each other, but she just kept getting more and more nervous. I didn't want her to get so scared that she'd never want to come out hunting again, so I explained that it was just something that hogs did and it was nothing to get concerned about. I told her we'd just cut the hunt short and head home. She said "no way, no how." She wasn't getting out of that stand with all that commotion going on all around us.

"Well what are we going to do?" I asked. "We can't stay here all night."

K.C. shook her head and said we were going to wait until they left or until I scared them off.

I nodded and said, "Okay, my dear."

So I stood up in the tree stand and started singing "Strangers in the Night" as loudly as I could. In about a nanosecond the entire woods went quiet. I took that as a compliment about my singing but K.C. suggested that they probably figured that if they stopped carrying on I would too. After a couple of verses, the hogs left the area so K.C. felt safe again, and we climbed out of the stand. We laughed all the way home and I can still get K.C. to laugh pretty much any time I want by bursting into my own unique rendition of Old Blue Eyes.

And then there's the hunting adventure that I recall as

a heartbreaker but K.C. remembers as a laughathon. I still hadn't killed anything in front of her to this point. We were about to hunt from a deer blind when I noticed that there was a branch obstructing one side of the blind. I decided to trim the branch so we'd have a clear view from all angles. K.C. didn't like to handle guns and she had absolutely no intention of shooting at anything. I was carrying a single-shot .243 Thompson. As a precaution, I took the bullet out, put it in my pocket and handed the rifle to K.C. I asked her to take it into the blind and lean it up against the side while I trimmed the branch. So I trimmed the branch and joined K.C. in the blind. She handed me the gun and we sat there waiting. Within a matter of minutes along came a little spike buck, walking down the hill. That caught my eye but what really captured my attention was the Godzilla buck following right behind. I'd been hunting this area for a long time, probably five or six years at that point, and this was the biggest whitetail I'd ever seen. This was in southern Georgia and this deer would have scored at least 160 inches. It was a really beautiful deer with a massive rack that spread way out past the ears. I mean this was a full-grown, boss-man of a buck. So, I picked up the gun and K.C. was really excited that we were finally going to harvest a deer together. I got him in the crosshairs quickly but I was real deliberate and patient. I kept my sight on him until I had it set up just perfect. I pulled the trigger, and ... *snap*! I had forgotten to put the bullet back in the chamber. The boss-man buck heard the hammer come down, looked over towards us and then turned around and walked off nice and calm like he knew he had all the time in the world. I, on the other hand, was shaking like a leaf. I was frantically trying to get the bullet out of my pocket, open the rifle, and get the bullet in place. By the time I was ready again, the deer was nowhere to be found. I turned towards K.C. and she had a look of total and complete shock. She didn't understand what had happened, so I told her I'd forgotten to reload the rifle.

She just felt so sorry for me and she was searching for something to say that would make me feel better.

"That deer was huge," she said with a half-grin. "Its butt was as wide as a horse!"

It was still too soon for me to see the humor in the moment. I mean it's rare to have an opportunity to get a buck that large and I was absolutely crushed. But I did enjoy seeing her amazement at the size of the animal, and it furthered her interest in joining me for additional hunts.

It wasn't until recently that I finally did harvest a deer in front of K.C. It was during black powder season in southern Florida. We were sitting together in the shooting house. K.C. has a really good eye and she watches intently for any sign of movement. She whispered to me that there was a doe walking through the field on her side of the house. I joined her there and saw a really nice 8-point buck trailing behind the doe. K.C. saw him too and got all excited. She moved aside so I could take aim, and I got off what I thought was a perfect shot. Because it was a muzzle-loader, all we could see was a big white cloud of smoke out the window. When I pulled the trigger I had caught a glimpse of the deer making a quick little turn into some tall grass so I was very confident that the deer was mortally wounded and would be easy to track down. I told K.C. we needed to sit still for a while and allow the deer time to bleed out and lie down to die. She was really excited but I assured her that waiting was the best way to make sure that we'd have a deer to dress and take home.

After a suitable time had passed, I told K.C. that I'd seen the deer take off after I hit him. She could come with me to that area and then wait there while I started looking for the deer's blood trail. So we got to the spot where I'd last seen the deer and, sure enough, I found some blood where the deer had bounded into the tall grass. That patch of tall grass turned out to be a thick cluster of myrtle bushes and other vegetation that was about six feet tall. I told K.C. it was going to be tough going in there and asked her to wait while I went in to get the buck. I found a good blood trail for the first twenty or thirty yards and then had to stop to figure out what direction he'd gone. All was quiet until I heard K.C.'s voice saying, "He went that way, he went that way." I turned around and saw K.C. right on my heels. She smiled and said, "I'm not missing out on this." Then she pointed out a blood splatter I had missed. Like I said earlier, K.C. has a really good eye and doesn't miss a thing. And that is a great skill for a hunter. Sometimes your only clue is a tiny drop of blood, a little bit of fur, or broken spider webs or branches. So K.C. gave me a nudge and we found the deer a few paces later. K.C. helped me haul the deer out of the woods and a couple of friends came by to help us get it into the truck and take it to the shop to be butchered. As we drove home with a cooler full of venison – all nicely cleaned and packaged – K.C. looked at me and said something that will always stay with me.

"I thought I was going to feel really sad and be upset," she said. "But I'm not. It was a good deer that lived a good life, and it died a good death. I'm very thankful for this harvest and it's a wonderful blessing for our family."

She proceeded to tell me how much all that red meat would have cost in the grocery store and how fortunate we were to have shared this experience. And it made me realize just how fortunate I was to have found such a wonderful woman to share my home life and my hunting life with.

Chapter 19

Unsung Heroes

When I was a kid my heroes were pretty typical – Batman, Grizzly Adams, and Bruce Lee. Today my heroes are largely unknown and unsung. They are the game wardens, rangers, conservation officers, and wildlife biologists who work tirelessly to protect our forests, plains, lakes, rivers, streams, coastal areas and all the creatures that live in those various habitats. They have one of the toughest and most under-appreciated jobs in the world; and to top it off, they're usually overworked and underpaid.

If you really want to get a sense of what these folks have to deal with, I'd recommend you read *Wildlife Wars*, written by Terry Grosz who served both as a California state fish and game warden and a special agent for the U.S. Fish and Wildlife Service. In the preface to the book, Grosz lists some of the rigors and obstacles endured by his profession:

> *...long hours, lousy food, dangerous animals, inclement weather, poor supervision, budgets designed to not allow one to do the job one was trained to do, national politics skewed towards private interests, wildlife that*

would not cooperate, equipment purchased from the lowest bidder, unsympathetic government attorneys, juries that did not have an ounce of common sense, judges who had no sense of history, more long hours, crooked state politics, useless state and federal help, and many more obstacles.

I like to describe fish and game wardens as the animals' police force. They're the ones who stop the lobster poachers from Florida all the way to Maine. They protect the bass in Lake Okeechobee and the trout in the streams of Colorado from greedy fishermen who exceed daily limits or keep undersized fish. And they stop the idiots who shine their car headlights into the woods or use spotlights to freeze deer and then shoot them. None of these people are hunters, fishermen or outdoorsmen. They're outlaws and criminals. They have no love or respect for wildlife or the treasure of our natural resources. These people are animals themselves. These are the people who trespass on private property. They drive along country roads at night with spotlights – intent on killing not hunting. They don't know how to hunt. They're cheaters and scumbags. And they give law-abiding hunters and fishermen a bad name. Left on their own, they would devastate our wildlife with their illegal and unethical poaching. And that's why I thank God for the men and women who continually monitor and police our woods and waterways.

While I believe the vast majority of people share my disgust with poachers, there are some people – including law-abiding hunters and fishermen – who criticize wardens for being too tough and not showing leniency. My view is totally the opposite. I say they're tough because they're doing their job well, and they aren't "lenient" because they take their responsibilities seriously. What I find particularly interesting about this issue is that law-abiding citizens never criticize police officers for being unbending about the law. If someone robs a store or assaults another person, he'll be arrested. No questions asked. It should be the same way with our wildlife. If someone shoots a deer out of season or keeps undersized striped bass, they should be arrested and charged with a crime. Because it is a criminal act. Responsible hunters would never kill a doe with a couple of young fawn trotting alongside of her. The fawn wouldn't survive without their mother and so the killing of one deer turns into the killing of three deer. Nonetheless, poachers do it without a second thought. Similarly, the keeping of undersized fish will harm the natural replenishment of the species. Poachers are the lowest of the low and I hate them with a purple passion. Anyone who owns or leases a piece of land – and has seen what poachers can do when they trespass – will understand exactly what I mean.

The need for Federal and state oversight of our forests, waters, and wildlife was recognized well over a century ago. It started with the appointment of a Commissioner of fish and fisheries to prosecute abuses and recommend protective and precautionary measures to Congress. This was followed a short while later by the creation of similar watchdog departments to monitor America's birds, mammals and plant life. The U.S. Fish and Wildlife Service as we know it today came into existence in 1940.

I know that there's a lot of discussion and controversy about the need for many of the governmental regulations that affect American businesses and individuals. And while I share many of the concerns about over-regulation, that is not – absolutely not – an issue when it comes to the oversight and protection of our natural resources and wildlife. Unspoiled land and healthy and abundant wildlife would disappear without the work of our fish and game agencies. Here's a factoid if you don't believe that. Today, in 2011, there are more deer in America than ever before. Most Americans – even those who are smarter than a fifth-grader – don't realize that. And the same is true of many animal species.

During the Great Depression people killed and ate pretty much any living creature they could find. Even raccoons were nervous during the Depression. Everything was being hunted because people couldn't afford to eat, and hungry people lived off the land. I know a lot of old people and old farmers who tell me about their childhood when they would regularly eat muskrat, possum, and squirrels. My own great-grandfather supported his family up in Ohio with a 22-caliber short and would feed his wife and kids with whatever he could get. Our natural wildlife were few and far between during and after the Depression. So it's no coincidence that the U.S. Fish and Wildlife Service came into its own in 1940. Something was desperately needed if America was going to be a land of both free people and free animals. The Service initiated major stocking programs for all kinds of animals all around the country. It wasn't something that could change overnight but would require decades of study and monitoring. When I was a kid up in Ohio it was a very rare and exciting event to see a deer. Today – even in more urban states like New Jersey – deer are seen everywhere. Unfortunately, deer are often seen as carcasses on the side of the road where they got the worst of a collision with a car or truck.

People don't realize that a herd of deer will typically double in size every year. So a state that has 500,000 deer will have one million the next year, and two million the year after that. And that's pretty much what happened all over the country starting in the years after the Depression. There was an explosion in the population of deer and many wildlife species – fueled by the proactive efforts of the wildlife agencies. Those efforts were accompanied by the massive post-war construction boom of the 1950s and 60s that continues to this day. The rise of suburban communities brought people closer to the natural habitat of animals and brought the animals closer to the homes, workplaces and playgrounds of American families. In many respects it was a recipe for disaster for both humans and animals, and it made the work of the wildlife services professionals even more critically important.

Another thing most people don't realize about the fish and game agencies is that they don't just protect our lands and wildlife, they also proactively purchase private lands. In the state of Florida, for example, the fish and game commission has used some of the money received from fishing and hunting licenses over the years to purchase land for public hunting and wildlife management. These properties are part of the five million acres of natural resource land managed by the Florida Fish and Wildlife Conservation Commission. Biologists assist in developing management plans, monitoring the animals on each property, and recommending how many hunters to allow, where they can hunt and what they can hunt. These management lands are wonderful places with a variety of terrains. Perhaps most importantly, because they are state-managed they provide a good source of protein for the many low-income people that live in rural parts of the state. These management lands are designed for the use and enjoyment of everyone, and many states have similar programs.

The bottom line is that the smartest and most effective way to show your love for animals is to support your local fish and game agencies. In Florida and probably in some other states, it's illegal to donate money directly to the fish and game agencies. But many states have independent associations like the Wildlife Foundation of Florida that do accept contributions and use those funds to support specific programs and projects.

But the number one thing that everyone who loves animals and our natural heritage should do – even if they don't hunt or fish – is to buy an annual hunting and fishing license. That money goes right towards helping the fish and game agencies stop poaching, monitor animal populations, hire biologists, and protect our beautiful American landscape. It's a small donation but it will make a meaningful difference to the world that you and your children will enjoy.

Chapter 20

An Open Letter to PETA

I learned at a very early age that if you don't have anything good to say about someone then you shouldn't say anything at all. I've strived to live my life along those lines, but experience has taught me that sometimes you do need to speak your mind. When those occasions arise, I force myself to keep it civil and polite. I don't like all the name-calling and downright slander that's taken over our political system, and I don't want to be a party to that kind of mean-spirited discussion. So this here is my open letter to the folks at the PETA (People for the Ethical Treatment of Animals) organization.

Dear PETA Members,

I'm sure you mean well. And I know you and I have a lot in common. We both love animals and want them to be treated with respect. We both agree that the world would be a lesser place if we didn't get to share it with all of God's creatures. And we agree that activities like dog-fighting and cock-fighting are barbaric and should be outlawed.

We also disagree on a lot – a real lot – of issues. But before I get into that, I'd like to ask a simple question: Have you ever taken a close look at your own advertising? It's sexist and offensive. The only theme that ties your ads together is a parade of half-naked women (with the occasional guy thrown in to be politically correct) and sexual innuendo. While your "Do Anglers Have Small Rods?" anti-fishing campaign is distasteful on every level, the prize for your worst ad has to go to the television spot where a pant-less Pamela Anderson is working as an airport security guard. She completely undresses her first customer, a ripped-torso male, because he was wearing a leather belt (which she tosses away with a look of disgust). The rest of the travelers are subjected to the same kind of nonsensical strip-downs, culminating with a totally naked couple walking through the metal detector. I know that sex sells, but this is absolutely absurd. And what's truly amazing is that an organization that is against the exploitation of animals can't seem to stop itself from exploiting Pamela Anderson's chest, Alicia Silverstone's rear-end, and Khloe Kardashian's hardbody curves. Even if someone were naive enough to agree with PETA's philosophy, they should view these ads as an indication of the organization's integrity and credibility – or lack thereof.

In addition to your tasteless ads, you seem to love in-your-face publicity stunts that also display your total lack of human decency. How could any decent person justify throwing red paint on people who wear fur coats? Even worse, how can anyone condone the brainwashing of young children by distributing books with titles like "Your Mommy Kills Animals!" and leaflets that trash American companies like your "McCruelty: I'm Hatin' It" campaign against McDonald's. Pitting children against their parents is reprehensible.

But let me get to the core of my disagreement with your mission. PETA is focused on "animal liberation." So instead of helping to ensure that animals are treated with dignity and respect, you believe that any use of any animal is immoral. Why? Because you believe that there is no fundamental difference between humans and the cows, chickens, fish, and other animals we share this world with. And that borders on insanity.

Your organization doesn't study animals and you don't live with animals. When you talk, you talk pie-in-the-sky theory. People like me, on the other hand, have literally spent years of our lives in the woods. When I was young I'd spend a whole day in the woods from sunrise to sunset. And I still do it occasionally today. I know how animals live in the wild because I've seen it with my own eyes. I've seen how they work together and how they fight. And animals do fight like hell against each other. It's part of the natural cycle – as is hunting. PETA will complain that when a hunter shoots an arrow into a deer, the deer is going to suffer. But you conveniently ignore what happens during rutting season. That's when the real suffering happens in the deer world. And it would be worse if there were no hunting. If the buck population soars – as it would without hunting – there would be thousands of smaller bucks who would be gored and sliced and suffer far more than from a well-aimed arrow or bullet. And remember, when these bucks go at each other, it's horn to horn, rack to rack. Sometimes the racks get so intertwined that the deer can't get loose and they both die in a tangled mess. I've even seen a picture of three bucks who got their horns all tangled up together and all three were found dead on a creek bed. Given the choice, I bet those dead bucks would have greatly preferred a hunter's bullet.

I also bet that a deer would much prefer a bullet to getting hit by a car. And if I were in charge of PETA (want to hire me?), that's where I would focus my attention. I did some research on this and came across some truly astounding figures. State Farm insurance estimates that in the twelve months ended June 30, 2010, there were over one million automobile collisions involving deer. These accidents resulted in over $4 billion of insurance claims and driver costs. State Farm calculates the average claim per accident at $3,100 plus a $250 deductible cost incurred by the drivers. To top it off, the National Highway Traffic Safety Administration says that deer-vehicle collisions during that same time period resulted in the deaths of 140 people. No one knows how many of the million-plus deer died as a result of these collisions – but those that died were the lucky ones. The deer that were only maimed struggled their way back into the woods to die a painful death, be killed by bobcats or mountain lions, or eaten alive by coyote or wolves. Now I know I'm a simple guy without a Harvard education, but it sure seems to me that this is an issue that deserves your attention. Perhaps you could stop criticizing people for owning pets – that are often treated way better than people – and actually do something to help animals. You spend way more time and money yelling at people than you do helping animals in need.

How about replacing one of your "leather belts are evil" ads with a campaign that asks, "How many dogs have you run over?" I ask that question a lot when I'm educating people, and almost everyone shakes their head and says "None. It would break my heart if I ever killed a dog." That's a good response—and people should feel the same way about deer, squirrels, raccoons, and so on; but they don't. Do deer suffer less than dogs when their legs get crushed by a car? How about rabbits or possum? If a million deer get hit by a car every year, I bet you're talking tens of millions of other creatures. Down here in Florida where I live, I know that snakes and turtles have a hard time getting across roads and many species are dying off. This is a huge issue, and I don't know what the answer is. But then again, I don't have the resources of your organization. I do know that people need to be more much aware when they're driving and slow down for any animal – whether it's a frog, chipmunk or deer. And that's something you can help educate people about.

But you can do something even more important. America is crisscrossed with superhighways, and many animals now have no safe route to wander and explore their natural territory. I'd love to see you folks focus on funding and advocating for fences along major crossing zones as well as bridges or tunnels to allow cougars, elk, bear and all their friends to pass safely from one side to the other. That would certainly support your goal of "animal liberation."

Now let me get to the heart of my disagreement with your mission. If you truly loved animals, you *would support hunters. Hunters have done way more than PETA to ensure that people and animals can co-exist in the modern world. In fact, I can say with confidence that if there were no hunters there wouldn't be any wildlife to hunt. The same thing goes for recreational fishermen. For example, Trout Unlimited is a cold-water conservation group with over 140,000 members. Each year, this group donates 500,000 hours and millions of dollars to clean local streams and rivers and help restore natural passageways and habitat. Ducks Unlimited is a similar organization whose 750,000 members are focused on conserving and restoring America's wetlands for the benefit of our waterfowl population. And closest to my heart are the efforts of the Quality Deer Management Association (QDMA) and its focus on ensuring a high-quality and sustainable future for our white-tailed deer population.*

Why don't you join forces with hunters and fishermen instead of attacking us as cruel misfits? Why don't you embrace a policy of peaceful co-existence instead of mortal combat? Why don't you follow the example of other conservation and animal advocate organizations? The Pennsylvania chapter of the National Audubon Society encourages its members to "Support deer hunting, even if you don't like the idea. In the long run it's the only humane solution and the only way to protect the native ecosystems that deer are part of and depend on."

And before you collect a single additional dollar in donations, why don't you remind potential donors that your president and co-founder, Ingrid Newkirk, is on record for stating that "Even if animal experiments did result in a cure for AIDS, of which there is no chance, I'd be against it on moral grounds."

Well you know what? I'm against PETA on moral grounds – and I think I'm on a lot firmer ground than you are.

Respectfully,
Mark Shepard

Section Three:

Coming Full Circle

MARK SHEPARD

Chapter 21

My Northern Exposure

I was about twenty-five years old when I left Florida and headed up to my childhood home back in Ohio and where my dad had settled after he and my mom got divorced. It was something I had been thinking about doing for a long time. I had only seen my father once since he'd left Florida when I was just ten. We'd talked occasionally on the phone, and he'd tell me what he was up to. He always ended the calls by saying that he loved me and missed me, but the reality was that it's impossible to maintain a relationship of any substance by long-distance telephone. My dad didn't know me and I didn't know him. And I wanted to change that and build a stronger and more meaningful connection between us.

The good news is that we spent about eight years together and we were able to build a powerful bond. My dad owned a country bar up in Collinsville, Ohio near Miami University. Despite its proximity to the campus, the bar mainly attracted a crowd of country folks and farmers. That bar was the centerpiece of my dad's life and he was content to spend most of his waking hours hanging out there, sitting on a barstool and trading stories with his customers. He was happy and, in the end, that's all any of us want so I guess it's great that he found the one thing that made him happy.

Hanging around bars has never been something I enjoy. I've always loved the outdoors; but in all the years I spent in Ohio, my dad never felt he could get away from his business long enough to go fishing or hunting with me. To his credit, however, he recognized my passion and introduced me to a bunch of old farmers who invited me to hunt or fish on their land. Through my dad's connections, I also met some people who were avid archers. I joined the local archery club and learned tips and techniques that greatly improved my skills and, to this very day, contribute to my effectiveness as a bow hunter.

When I first arrived in Ohio, I lived in a one-room apartment in the back of dad's bar. The bar itself was part of a big L-shaped building with a nightclub, dance hall and poolrooms. The bar was situated on seven acres surrounded by cornfields. There was a gas station on one side of it and a graveyard across the street. Other than that it was pretty much in the middle of nowhere with nothing but farmland and forests for miles.

Because the bar was so isolated – and it would take the sheriff's department at least thirty minutes to respond to a call – it attracted a fair share of burglars and mischief-makers who figured it was an easy target. I remember one incident, in particular, that really got my adrenaline flowing. It was about three or four o'clock in the morning, and the bar was closed. My dad and I were sitting at the bar when a guy tiptoed up to the side door. We could see him out the window, but he couldn't see us. He was a big guy and he started working on the door trying to get it open. My dad whispered to me to go get my .44 Magnum that I kept in the back room.

When I got back, my dad was shaking his head as he

watched the guy working his ass off trying to bust the lock. He was determined to get into the building; and, considering how many crazy psychopaths there are in the world, it was a really spooky situation. Because it would take so long for law enforcement to get there, we figured we'd handle the situation ourselves. My dad outlined the game plan. He said he would reach over and quietly unlock the door. He reminded me that the door swung outwards. He said when the guy opens the door, I want you lay that .44 right across his freakin' head and blast a round right over the top of his head. And then he paused and whispered an order: "*Do not* shoot the eave." And he kept repeating it – "Do not hit the building." He wasn't too concerned about what I did with the guy, but he sure didn't want me to hit the building. I nodded and positioned myself next to the door.

We both understood that, in addition to the element of surprise, we had an advantage in that there was a light in the parking lot so we'd be able to see okay; but the bar interior would look pitch black to the burglar. So my dad reached over and unlocked the door. After a brief moment, the guy figured he had finally unlocked the door and slowly pulled it open. Just like my dad had planned it, I laid that .44 Magnum – with its 11-inch barrel – about a foot away from his ear and I let it rip. I aimed way above his head shooting into the cornfield and far away from the building's eaves. Now, in addition to a loud blast, a .44 Magnum throws out a pretty long flame that captured the guy's expression of terror. I can't know for sure exactly what went through his mind at that moment, but I'm absolutely sure that he couldn't hear out of one side of his head for a few days. It took him a second to figure out what had happened and then he took off running. And that's when the real fun began. There's a beer garden behind my dad's bar. It's surrounded by a six-foot wooden fence and includes a volleyball court, horseshoe pits and barbeque equipment. Behind the fence is a pile of debris that's been building up for upwards of fifty years. It's nothing but scrap lumber with rusty nails, bricks and jagged chunks of concrete, and broken whiskey bottles. So this would-be-burglar started hauling ass through the beer garden and he ran right into the volleyball court. And that's a sight that I'll never forget and still gets me laughing today. The guy hit the volleyball net at full speed and clotheslined himself. He got flung backwards and landed hard on his back. We were yelling at him to get the hell off our property or we'd blow his brains out, so he hopped back up and climbed over the fence. He landed in that pile of trash and we could hear him screaming as he was punished by the nails, shards of glass and other sharp-edged debris. He finally made it to the cornfields and disappeared. I suspect that was the end of his burglary career.

In addition to my dad's bar, the only other local business that could attract thieves was the BP gas station. The owner had tricked out the station with surveillance cameras both inside and out, but that didn't always serve to frighten away burglars. And because the station was right next to the bar, we often had a front-row view of the shenanigans. The best incident happened one night after the bar was closed. I happened to walk past the window and saw three guys up on the roof of the station. I called my dad over to check out the scene. He rolled his eyes and told me to get the .44 while he went to call the sheriff. We both came back to the window and watched these idiots go about their business. Their plan was to tear off the vent that sat atop the roof and then drop down the opening into the convenience store, empty the cash register and steal everything that wasn't nailed down. Well, after a lot of banging with hammers and crowbars, they did manage to remove the vent but they also did a lot of damage to the roof and exposed all the ductwork that was tucked up under the roof. One of the guys tried to squeeze through an opening between the ducts and the hole where the vent had been. He slipped and fell. We found out later that he fell onto a joist, right on his pelvis, and both legs went through the dry wall ceiling. My dad and I could hear the guy screaming and then his two buddies started trying to pull him back up. My dad looked at me with a grin and said it's time to have some fun. "So you want me to do it," I asked. He nodded and told me to go for it. I opened the window and unloaded that .44 into the sky about fifty feet over their heads. They could certainly hear those .44 rounds zipping right above them, they could probably feel the whoosh as the bullets sped by, and they could see the frightening flash of blue from my gun as I fired. So, at this point, these three guys are pretty much wetting all over themselves. They jumped off the roof – which had to be especially painful for the guy who'd fallen through the dry wall. They ran across the street and into the graveyard. They must have had the foresight to leave their car in the graveyard, and they came flying out with the gas pedal floored and their lights out. We were able to identify what kind of car it was and saw that they were headed north on Route 127.

The sheriff showed up about half an hour later and the burglar alarm, which had been triggered when the guy fell through the ceiling, was still screeching. We explained to the two officers what had happened – except for the part about me unloading the .44 above their heads. We described the car and told them that it was headed north towards Somerville. Now I still have some friends in Somerville, and I don't want to insult anyone; but Somerville is a classic hillbilly community with maybe 75 houses in the whole town. I've heard it's where they invented the toothbrush, because if it had been invented anywhere else it would have been the "teethbrush." I mean these are deep-country backwoods people. If they want a date, they go to the family reunion. I literally – and this is no exaggeration – remember seeing some Somerville dudes pulling out each other's teeth with a pair of pliers. So anyway, the police headed up to Somerville and they saw a parked car that matched the description we'd given them. One of the policemen got out, put his hand on the hood of the car, and felt that it was hotter than Georgia asphalt. Since it was about four o'clock in the morning at this point, and no one else was out and about, he figured he had a likely suspect. So he rang the doorbell and a kid of about 19 or 20 answers. The sheriff asked him if he and his buddies had been out riding around. The kid shook his head and said, no, we've been here all night. The sheriff looked him up and down and saw that he had fiberglass insulation all over his clothes. So the sheriff said, I think you and your pals need to come out here and talk. Within a couple of minutes the three guys were handcuffed and on their way to the local jail. Busted! And my dad and I had done our civic duty for the day.

In both of these situations, I aimed the gun above and away from the burglars. But there was one time when I was shooting to kill because my life – and my dad's life – was truly in danger. It was another early morning when my dad and I were sitting at the bar after having finished cleaning up after the last customers had left. It was as quiet as the proverbial church mouse. All of a sudden we heard a shotgun blast coming from the back of the building. The buckshot blew out a lighted beer sign and totally destroyed the window that looked out over the rear parking lot. We heard glass flying everywhere, and quickly got down behind the bar. At that point we didn't know who was shooting at the bar or what they wanted, but we acted instinctively. I stayed down low and crawled around the corner into the apartment, grabbed a Ruger 10/22 rifle and my trusty .44 Magnum. I gave the 10/22 to my dad and tightly gripped my .44. We peeked up over the top of the bar and saw the flash from another shotgun blast. This was bad. Really bad. And so we just opened fire aiming in the general direction of where the shotgun blast had come from. We didn't have a clue who or what we were up against, but we had to defend ourselves. It was clear that whoever these people were, their plan was to shoot first and ask questions later, so we took on the same attitude. After we emptied our rounds we loaded up again, but we were surrounded by silence. Either the crazy people were setting a trap and hoping we would open the door to see if they were still around, or we'd managed to scare them off. The sheriff decided that the latter was the case and that they had gotten away on foot and then escaped in a waiting car or truck. He also determined that someone had been hit with a bullet. He couldn't tell how badly the guy had been hurt, but there was a definite blood trail to where the getaway vehicle must have been waiting. The sheriff's department contacted every hospital in the area to see if anyone had been admitted for a gunshot wound, but nothing ever panned out.

I remember thinking at the time that I was a good Christian who believed in forgiveness, but I had a real hard time feeling any forgiveness. I was pissed. To the point that if they had found a dead body, I'd have wanted my picture taken with it like a trophy shot. I couldn't imagine how someone could do something like that. As far as they knew, they might have been shooting at women or little children who happened to be in the wrong place at the wrong time. You read about that kind of thing happening in big cities like New York where a little kid gets caught in a cross fire and dies from a bullet through his head or chest. It's evil. And so the evil guy or guys who shot at my dad's bar were never found. When the sheriff questioned us about the particulars and whether there was anyone who might be looking for revenge, we told them that there had been a fight in the bar earlier in the evening and we'd had to tell the parties to leave. But that happens pretty often in bars, so I don't know, and I'll never know, if that was the cause for the attack. What I do know is that it was a terrifying experience.

I've always loved my dad's spirit. He's a tough old ex-Marine, but he was just as scared as I was; and I don't think either of us slept a wink for nights. The sheriff's department up there was very good to us and they stationed a deputy out in front of the bar every night for a couple weeks. I guess the moral of the story is that our guns saved our lives. I know a lot of people don't like and disagree with the NRA slogan that "Guns Don't Kill People, People Kill People;" but to my mind the better quote is that "Guns Protect the People that People Try to Kill." Because if we didn't have our weapons handy, I wouldn't be around to write this book and my dad wouldn't be around to enjoy his grandchildren.

I don't want to leave the impression that my time in Ohio was like the Wild West, with nothing but shoot-outs and bad guys wearing black hats. My dad and I had a lot of quiet and peaceful times together. And I also spent a lot of time bass fishing and refining the skills that would one day allow me to join the professional bass fishing circuit. I worked for long time as a bartender for the Fraternal Order of the Eagles, and the folks there treated me really well. I made a lot of friends and earned a reliable and steady income for the first time in my life.

The bottom line is that my time in Ohio was very special and meaningful, especially after something happened when I least expected it. But that's a story for another chapter (the next, *hint hint*).

Chapter 22

Soul Brothers

My brother and I have been inseparable for our whole lives. To say we love each other like the brothers we are would be a gross understatement. It's almost like we're twins who were born two years apart. Chris and I have the same outlook on life and we enjoy the same activities. We also always enjoyed tormenting each other and beating the crap out of each other just for the fun of it.

Admittedly we grew up in a different time. Today, kids can't get into a normal neighborhood scuffle without somebody calling 9-1-1. It's ridiculous. Fights and tussles are a normal part of growing up. I'm not talking about bullying, which is a terrible problem in our society, but rather the harmless wrestling and shoving matches that actually help kids learn about the character of different people – as well as their own character. I believe deeply that a kid who doesn't learn how to stand up for himself will have a hard time in this world.

Chris and I always understood the boundaries between right and wrong, but we'd push it sometimes. I remember one time we were walking to a local fishing pond.

We were carrying BB guns and fishing poles and, probably just to see what would happen, Chris aimed his BB gun and shot me in the butt. I had to go home and pull down my pants so my momma could get the BBs out of my butt. We used to do all kinds of stuff like that. He put me in the hospital, and I put him in the hospital.

There was one time, however, when we both went too far. It was a hot summer day and we'd just come back to the house with a couple of friends after fishing down at the pond. We had a basketball hoop in our driveway and I started shooting baskets. Chris grabbed the ball away from me, and he wouldn't let me play any more. I was mad and I said I was going to go back to the greenhouses where my grandma was and tell her what he had done. As I was walking away, Chris threw a rock at me and it came down right on top of my head. The thing split my head open and blood started pouring down my face. I ran the rest of the way to the greenhouse, and my grandma saw me covered in blood and panicked. She rushed me to the hospital and I had to get a dozen stitches. Plus the whole top of my head had to be shaved and I had to walk around with a giant bandage for weeks. It was really embarrassing for me, and people started calling me names and stuff, and I was getting madder and madder and I promised myself that I would get my revenge.

But first Chris had to get his butt whipped – first by my mother and then again by my dad when he got home from work. Chris knew it was coming, knew it was deserved and didn't try to fight it. He didn't threaten to call DSS, and no one who witnessed or heard his beating viewed it as child abuse. He was simply being held accountable for his actions.

So I waited for my opportunity for revenge to come around. A couple of weeks later, with my head still wrapped in bandages, I hid myself in some bushes just off a road where

I knew Chris would be bicycling. I'd found a chunk of asphalt about the size of a pie plate that had broken off the road and I held it tightly. I saw Chris coming and I timed my ambush perfectly. I ran right at him and slammed the asphalt on his hand where he was holding the handlebars. He flipped over the front of the bike and slid down the road. He ended up in the same hospital I'd gone to and he left wearing a cast to immobilize his broken hand. I got a whupping from my mom and dad, but the next day Chris and I were back to laughing and fishing together. We were brothers and we'd still get into fights with each other, but our love and loyalty for each other was never questioned. Because Chris was older than me, he often looked out for me. There were a couple of bullies in our neighborhood who unwisely chose me as one of their targets. Chris went after them and taught them the lesson that he was the only one allowed to beat his little brother's ass.

Chris and I grew up together and worked side-by-side as commercial fishermen, so it was a huge transition for both of us when I left Florida and moved to Ohio to spend some time with our dad. This was the first time we'd been apart for any extended period; and though we talked a lot by phone, it just wasn't the same. After I'd been in Ohio for about three years, Chris called me one day and said he was done with swordfishing. He'd just up and quit. We talked about how much we missed each other, and I suggested he could probably find some work up in Ohio if he wanted to. I heard Chris chuckle and he told me to step out the back door. I opened the door and there he was with his pickup truck and a U-Haul trailer. I tell you the tears flowed hot and heavy that day, and we haven't lived more than a few miles apart ever since.

It didn't take long for Chris to find work. Our dad's bar was the only game in town and everyone hung out there.

We got to know all the guys, and Chris met a fellow that had a well-drilling business and ended up going to work for him. So we both buckled down with our jobs, and started making decent money. I already had a bass boat, then Chris saved up enough money to buy himself a bass boat, and I bought myself an even nicer bass boat as I prepared myself for a professional fishing career. We started fishing the Redman Tournaments together while we were in Ohio. We hunted together and, in fact, we went back to doing exactly what we did as kids. It was a fun time for both of us.

It also turned out to be one of the most painful periods of my life. I'd always been a hard worker. I did a lot of steel work and carpentry as well as the brutally hard labor associated with commercial fishing. Over the years I had built up calcium on my elbow, all the tendons in my forearm were messed up, and I had an aneurism in the palm of my hand. The pain was excruciating. Two fingers on my left hand were always numb and I felt like a golf ball was jammed in my armpit. To top it off, I felt like I was having a heart attack all the time. I went to one doctor after another trying to get the problem diagnosed and fixed. The good news was that I had excellent health insurance from the Eagle, so I didn't have to worry about going bankrupt. The doctors did all kinds of tests, injecting me with dyes and taking MRIs and CAT scans from every conceivable angle. No one could find anything until I met this one little Indian doctor who did some electrical tests on my nerves. He told me he'd found something, and I almost cried right there in front of him. I prayed that he was right because I was running out of patience and I was hurting so bad I was about ready to shoot myself. The doctor sent me to a hand surgeon at the University of Cincinnati who did a lot of work with professional ballplayers. I drove to the UC medical center and met Dr. Stern. We hit it off immediately. I told him I was a pro fisherman but couldn't compete anymore because of the pain. He assured me that he would do everything in his power to get me competing again. He ran a bunch more tests and discovered the problem. He said he'd never seen anyone with an aneurism on the palm before and that we were going to make medical history together. And then he said that the surgery wouldn't cost me a nickel – not even the deductible. He said he would do all the required surgeries for free as long as he could bring in some colleagues and students to observe. I told him he could bring in a marching band as long as he could fix me up. The surgery went off without a hitch. They took all the skin off my elbow and forearm and re-routed my funny bone nerve. They fixed up my elbow so it's practically as good as new – and I've got the scar tissue from literally hundreds of stitches and staples to remind me of the miracle of modern medicine. Then they cut open my hand from between my pinkie and index finger, all the way down to my wrist. They removed the aneurism and did some additional nerve work in my hand.

The relief was almost instantaneous. The pain in my chest was gone. The golf ball in my armpit was gone, and I knew it would only be a matter of time before I'd be able to fish again and start competing in tournaments. I had a full cast from my shoulder to my hand, with my arm in a sling; and it would take a whole year for me to fully heal. But there was light at the end of the tunnel and I was ready to shine like never before.

I was never one to be content sitting around the house. My whole life had been lived on the go, but here I was unable to work and under doctor's orders to refrain from anything even remotely physical. I know I would have gone absolutely bonkers if Chris hadn't been around. And having

Chris there helped both of us come to major decisions about the rest of our lives.

Chris and I had always talked a lot, but our conversations took on a deeper and more urgent vibe during my recovery from surgery. I told Chris I wanted to keep fishing professionally and that it was time to swing for the fences. I didn't want to stand behind a bar serving drinks for the rest of my life. There had to be more to life than that. Chris just kept nodding his head like one of those bobble-head dolls, and said, "You took the words right out of my mouth. I don't want to drill wells the rest of my life either. I like the work, but it'll kill you as you get older. It's brutal work. Plus," he said, "I *like* it, but I *love* fishing."

So, like the soul brothers we always were, we came to the same decision at the same time. We were going to live life to the fullest. We'd move back to Florida, get jobs as fishing guides, and see how far we could go with professional bass fishing. It was hard to say goodbye to our dad, after we'd just reconnected with him, but it was now or never time and we had to move on.

As soon as my cast was removed and the doctor gave me the thumbs-up, Chris, his newlywed wife, and I packed up everything we owned. We had a convoy of three pick-up trucks, one towing a U-Haul trailer and the other two pulling our bass boats. We had planned to keep the pedal to the metal all the way to Florida, but it turned out to be the trip from hell. We had just entered Kentucky when Chris' truck caught on fire. We're still not sure what happened, but something must have shorted or sparked and we're lucky the whole thing didn't blow up. After we got the fire extinguished and felt like it was safe to continue, we proceeded to burn out some bearings and crack an axle before we made it home to Florida. But we were home, and that's all that mattered.

******

Not too long after we were back in Florida, Chris and his wife had a child. It was a baby boy and they named him Mark. Everyone calls him "Little Mark Shepard." He's eleven years old now, and I'm still honored and humbled that Chris would name his first-born after me. It was the ultimate compliment and proof-positive that our relationship has always been and always will be one of unequivocal brotherly love.

Chapter 23

A Boy's Dream - A Man's Dream Come True

Moving back to Florida got me back near the ocean waters where I'd grown up. But I came back to Florida a different person than when I'd left. I had a renewed energy and a renewed determination to succeed as a professional bass fisherman. And I knew in my heart that my experience in Ohio would help me achieve my goals.

Like all kids I grew up with a dream of what I wanted to be. I didn't have the book-smarts to be a professional like a doctor or lawyer, and I didn't have the calling to be a police officer or fire fighter. What I had was a love of fishing and a lot of self-confidence that – with my natural ability combined with a lot of hard work – I'd be able to fish with the best fishermen in the world. I distinctly remember watching fishing shows and bass tournaments on television and, even though I didn't know how to go about getting there, I knew that was my one true passion. As I got older I realized that I needed to greatly expand my horizons if I hoped to have any success in the major tournaments. I needed to visit and fish a much wider variety of waters, climates and habitats. Growing up in South Florida, we primarily fished in grass, shallow waters and swamps. Pro bass fishermen, however, have to able to succeed in rivers, deep-water lakes, in cold waters and warm, and in still waters and rushing waters. You had to be able to understand all kinds of totally different terrains and adapt your equipment and technique to whatever the tournament gods threw your way. Living in Ohio gave me that opportunity and I grabbed that bull by the horns and never let go. When I wasn't working, I'd pick out a lake on the map and drive all over Ohio and into Tennessee and Kentucky and do nothing but fish for two or three days. I often slept in my pickup truck because I didn't have a whole lot of money, and what I had I much preferred to spend on new fishing equipment. It was also during those fishing trips that I started hand-carving and painting balsa crank baits to help fill in the quiet times after the sun set. It's a hobby that I still enjoy and some of the lures I designed ended up being manufactured and sold to other fishermen.

Some of the very best fishermen that I ever met lived in Ohio, and I had the good fortune to learn from them. These friendships also led to me being invited to join a bass club and that's how I got my first taste of tournament fishing. These were just local tournaments but they were a lot of fun and got me exposed to the mindset and preparation you need to succeed in competition.

Back in those days, the Bassmasters Tour was the big dog of pro bass fishing. The Red Man Tournament Trail, sponsored by Red Man chewing tobacco, was more open and accessible to new participants. Nowadays, Walmart has taken over name sponsorship of this tournament; but I know for a fact that most of the guys who are touring today with Bassmasters got their start with the Red Man. The Red Man was a fantastic event. It allowed new entrants to participate ether as a boater or a non-boater who got paired up with a boater. The tournament was divided by region and state and allowed you to fish alongside some of the biggest names in the business. Living in Ohio, I competed in the Buckeye Division. But before I was ready to compete, I needed to upgrade my boat to something bigger that could handle some of the rougher water I'd be facing. So I traded up to an 18-foot Ranger with a 175-hp Mercury. That 361 Ranger was a great fishing boat – nice riding and super fast – but, as I found out later, it was still a little small for the conditions that Lake Erie and other large lakes could deliver.

I entered my first Red Man tournament and was rightly nervous about going up against 150-200 of the best anglers in Ohio. I was confident that my mechanics were good, but I knew I had a lot to learn about technique. I was real green – a realization that was brought home as I talked with and observed my more seasoned competitors. Nonetheless, I stayed focused and succeeded far beyond anything I could have imagined. I finished sixteenth and received a check. I got paid for bass fishing and I was giddy with excitement. I ended up earning a couple more checks that season, and I finished my rookie year in the Buckeye Division in seventeenth place. That qualified me for a regional tournament in North Carolina which was a huge deal because when you fished in a regional tournament, you were fishing for a brand new boat, a truck and a chance to go to the All-American. I didn't expect to win, but at least I had a chance. And that's all I ever wanted. So I went to North Carolina, and I didn't do very well; but I had nothing to complain about. By every standard of measure, my first season was a thrill-a-minute success.

The following season, I thought I would try both of

the local Red Man divisions: the Buckeye and the Hoosier. The first Buckeye Division tournament of the year was on Lake Erie, and I found out just how scary it can be trying to pilot an undersized bass boat during severe weather conditions. We were launching out of Sandusky Bay and, as we waited, we were being pelted by gale force winds. I could see five- and seven-foot waves out in the bay and there were rescue boats situated all around the lake in case someone got in serious trouble. I thought for sure they would cancel the tournament, but they started calling out our numbers and launching us one at a time. I briefly considered withdrawing – and that would have been the intelligent thing to do – but I was still new at this game and didn't want to tick off the event organizers. The other factor that led me to stay in the tournament despite the weather was that I had a lot of confidence in myself as a boat operator. I'd worked in the Atlantic Ocean with small boats riding breakers. I knew how to ride waves and read the water. And I'd flipped a couple of boats in my day.

Now let's pause for a moment, and consider what I've just admitted. *I'd flipped a couple of boats in my day.* To some people that admission would be the kiss of death. They'd be nervous about going out on a boat with me. I mean given the choice between a captain who has flipped a boat and another captain who's never flipped a boat, most folks would choose the guy with the unblemished record. But most folks would be wrong. I know that I'm a better captain because of my accidents. I know my limitations and the limitations of my boat. A guy that's never flipped a boat and experienced the extremes of what can happen on the water is much more likely to take a risk and see how far he can push luck against nature. So, if you're ever faced with that choice, go with the guy who's looked death in the eye rather than one who's only read about it.

So, we're back on Lake Erie. It's still pitch dark and it's as spooky a morning as I've ever seen. They continued calling the boats out one at a time at a nice steady pace, slowing them when it got too congested. I kept looking out over the water and it was some nasty slop. By the time my number got called, I'd decided to just take my time and slowly chip away at these big old nasty waves with my small Ranger boat. I focused on keeping the bow up, but ahead of me I saw a bunch of guys trying to jump across the tops of waves. Before I was even out into open water, I saw two boats flip upside down and the rescue boats hurried over trying to get the guys out of the water. As I slowly made my way out, I saw another boat flip and a few others stalled out and filled with water. There was even one boat – a cheaply made boat that never should have been out on Lake Erie in the first place – that went down and sunk to the bottom. I finally made it out of the bay and into the main lake and, no exaggeration, it looked like the gates of hell with giant ground seas ready to toy with our minds and machines. I started to set a course down to the reef where I wanted to go fish. I was slowly walking my way through these huge waves. The technique was to drop down into the trough and then roll up on the sides, and just keep rolling them out. There were several boats doing the same thing and we were doing our best to keep an eye on each other, but it's hard to see when one boat is down in the trough and another is on top of a wave. And that's when bad things happen. I was just starting to climb up a wave when I saw another boat trying to climb the wave above me on my starboard side. He couldn't see me and he was about to come down on top of me. The wave was already crashing down and water was coming into my boat. I had a millisecond to react and I gave it full throttle and shot up from underneath him. It terrified both of us, but

I had to put it behind me and start fishing.

I had only fished a couple of tournaments on Lake Erie, so I didn't know it as well as I did my home turf of Okeechobee. But there was an area near a reef that I liked so I settled down and drifted. The water was so rough and the boat was bobbing up and down so high that I wouldn't even attempt to stand up or put my trolling motor over. I just threw out a drift sock and sat on the deck of my boat. I dragged tubes most of the day and the fishing wasn't bad. I caught my limit and, at the end of the day when I got back in, there were still boats upside down, tied to the dock. I had survived but just barely, and I decided that my boat just wasn't big enough and my back wasn't strong enough for this kind of deal. All the days of commercial fishing and steel work had taken their toll on my spine. Getting tossed around in a bass boat is like being in the ring all day with an Ultimate Fighting Sumo wrestler. It's pretty brutal on the body. So I left the Buckeye Division and focused all my attention on the Hoosier Division.

The Hoosier hosts a lot of tournaments on the Ohio River, and that's a body of water that I've always loved. A lot of people complain that it's one of the worst fisheries in the world, but I think that's because it's such a challenging place to fish. One of the things I love about fishing the Ohio River is its natural beauty. It's absolutely breathtaking. The river is very big; and with all the tributaries flowing into it, you can go way up in the creeks and experience scenery that very few people have ever seen. The vastness of the Ohio also gives you a sense of freedom and wonder. Its landscapes vary from the hustle and bustle of cities like Cincinnati to remote wilderness areas and farm country. Part of my affection for the Ohio River probably stems from the fact that I was also pretty successful there. That year – which was only my second fishing in professional tournaments – I had one second-place finish and a bunch in the top ten, so I was collecting a steady stream of checks. The checks were small but they were still checks for good old American dollars. I finished fourth in the Hoosier Division that year and made the Regionals again.

One of the shortcomings in my fishing career was due to the fact that the Regional tournaments take place in the fall. I'd always had a hard time putting my boat in the water that time of year because that's when archery season opened and I wanted to be in a tree stand with my bow. I'd had a lot of time to learn about fall fishing in the northern country, but hadn't made the most of that opportunity. But that year, fishing at the Regional on Kentucky's Barkley Lake, I learned a ton about fall fishing and I felt like I was ready to take the Hoosier Division by storm the next season. But that wasn't to be. That's when my arm and hand pain got so severe that I had to go under the knife. I missed the whole season, but I also made the life-changing decision to move back to Florida.

Strictly from the standpoint of my fishing career, getting back to Florida was a huge plus for me. It put me back into what I consider my natural habitat – the swamps and heavy grass of Lake Okeechobee. The first time I saw that lake, I fell in love with it; and it's been my favorite playground ever since I was 10 years old. I had a ball growing up around Okeechobee, and I was delighted to be back home and excited to be able to compete in tournaments on my home turf. I landed a job that allowed me a lot of flexibility to train and compete and to take off whatever time I needed to tour as a pro fisherman.

Once I was fully recovered from my surgery, I got back into the swing of fishing and qualified for the EverStart Series, which is one of the professional tournament trails of the FLW. The EverStart was one of the less expensive big-time tournaments to compete in. Without having a corporate sponsor, I felt I could swing the entry fees and operating costs out of my own pocket. My plan was to take it one tournament at a time. I was fishing in the Southeast Division and I decided that if I earned a check from the first tournament, I'd enter the second one and take it from there. My first EverStart competition was on Okeechobee – my home away from home – and I had a great tournament finishing in twelfth place. I earned a nice check and was excited about competing against and holding my own against some of the best fishermen in the world.

The next stop was on Lake Eufaula, Alabama. A good friend of mine lived up that way and went out with me on my boat and showed me the layout of the lake. As we looked around and explored, it seemed like there were fish everywhere. Over the next few days of practice, I stayed close to Lakeport, where we launched, and found a massive school of fish hiding up in some thick bushes. I figured this tournament was going to be a slugfest and everybody was going to catch a lot of fish. As a result, I decided to stay close, maximize my fishing time, and concentrate on this one area. That's exactly what I did when the tournament started and I brought in a really nice sack the first day: 16 pounds even. The second day, I brought in another 16 pounds and made it into the top 30 of about 165 anglers. I knew I needed a little bit more weight to make the top ten, so I hit it a little harder. On day three I brought in 18 and a half pounds and jumped all the way up to fifth place. This was big-time fishing and I had a chance to earn my first big-time check. I was excited and nervous, but also confident and focused. I went to bed early and couldn't wait to wake up and hit the water.

Well the next day brought a torrential rainstorm, but I didn't have time to worry about getting wet. Victory was in sight and I wasn't going to waste a moment of it. I motored back to my fishing spot. It was up behind some bushes in a real shallow, marshy pond with tall trees all around us. The fishing was spectacular. I was crushing it even as the rain kept pouring down and lightning started to crack at a steady pace. I had a non-boating co-angler with me and he was getting scared to death. He kept saying, "We gotta get out of here; we gotta get out of here." I shook my head and told him that the good Lord wasn't ready for us. I said there was a lot at stake and we needed to hunker down and keep fishing. I knew he wasn't happy about it, but he kept fishing just like I said. Within a couple of minutes he landed a big old fish and started shouting to the heavens, "I believe! I believe." As the day went on, the fishing kept getting better and better. I noticed that the water level was coming up, so I was able to get farther back into this little marsh pond. We were all by ourselves in there and we started catching more and more big fish. And I mean *big*. I came in with a catch of 21 pounds and enjoyed my first big win. How big you might ask? How about $50,000 big? I pretty much jumped out of my skin. That was one of the biggest and most exciting moments of my life and it helped to further propel my pro fishing career.

Like I said earlier, Bassmasters represents the major leagues of pro fishing. My success in the EverStart campaign got me corporate sponsorships with Skeeter bass boats and Yamaha engines and that led to my rookie season on the Bassmasters trail. I had a lot of success in the 2003 Bassmasters Southern Open. It's a three-tournament, four-division trail with about 220 boats. And at the end of the trail, you had to be in the top 20 of your division to make the Southern Open Championship. And the 220 anglers in the 2003 Southern Open included all the legends in the business. We started out on Lake Wheeler in North Carolina. I did okay there and ended up in the middle of the pack. The next stop was Lake Eufaula back in Alabama. Eufaula has always been a good lake for me, and I did real well there. I earned a nice check and got my points up even more. The final competition was on my traditional stomping ground, Lake Okeechobee, in the fall. The weather and lake were rough; but the fishing was good, and I finished third. I was going against big-name competition and my third-place finish was nothing to be ashamed of. I was justifiably proud of my performance.

No chapter about fishing could be complete without a sob-story fishing tale about the one that got away. This is mine, and it still gives me nightmares. I had two monster fish on the line during that final Okeechobee tournament. And by monster I mean eight-pounders. Either one of them would have won me the tournament outright. The first one I have to chalk up to plain old bad luck. He ended up on top of a grass mat, and I couldn't get it to come to me. It eventually came off the hook, and then flip-flopped for a while before digging itself back down into the water. The other one, however, was lost due to what is politely referred to today as "user error." Not mine, but a user error on the part of my co-angler (whose name I won't share but he knows who he is!). I was fighting this monster fish around the boat, and I asked my co-angler to net him. He went and grabbed the net, and then stood there and did nothing. I had the fish right alongside the boat, and then it surged one more time and pulled off. I stared at the guy in disbelief and his only excuse was that he didn't know the way around my boat. To this day I still don't understand what he meant by that comment, but the guy cost me an eight-pound fish. Nonetheless, every pro has a handful of bad-luck stories. And the good news was that I felt truly blessed to finish third for the event – and that led to me finishing ninth for the whole division.

My high finish in the Southern Open earned me an invitation to the Open Championship at Toledo Bend Lake, bordering Texas and Louisiana. Because I'd finished in the top 15 of the Southern, I had an automatic qualification for the following year's Bassmasters Tour – but I didn't let that affect my focus or determination. I felt I was in a good zone and wanted to make the most of every opportunity. The Toledo Bend tournament took place in early December. The weather was cold and the lake was rough. That lake threw all kinds of different weather conditions and distinct bodies of water at us. The most unique day was spent on a section of the lake that had standing timber everywhere. When you looked across the lake, it looked like a million fence posts jutting out of the water. What made it especially memorable – and very scary – was the way the wind was whipping up swells that were six-feet high. I was motoring down to one of my fishing spots during the competition. There was a narrow boat lane right through these treetops, and the waves were driving me up and down like a rollercoaster. As I crested over a wave it looked like someone was trying to spear me on both sides of the boat. And then when I got to the trough, I felt like I was being caged in by all this big timber. It was nerve-wracking, but I finally got to my spot. I had a great tournament overall and placed thirteenth. Not bad for a rookie. So I collected a good paycheck and had my automatic qualification for the 2004 Bassmasters Tour. Life was good.

I started my Bassmasters rookie year less than two months later in late January. I have to admit that it was an intimidating experience, but I had the good fortune to start out with several other rookies who are now stars in their own right: Greg Hackney, Scott Suggs, Greg Pugh, and J.T. Kenny. J.T. and I did some traveling together and shared some expenses. It was a very hectic schedule traveling from one tournament to the next. I was gone for up to nine weeks at a time. But I was doing what I'd always dreamed of and loved every minute of it. It was a great learning experience for me. There were several times when I passed on fish thinking they weren't big enough, and I'd keep searching for the lunker that would make my day. But more often than not, I'd have done better if I'd stuck with the fish I released rather than the ones I caught after. It's all part of the learning process and understanding the waters you're fishing on and the psychology of competition. I can't lie and say that I lit the tour on fire, but I made a few checks and I re-qualified for the upcoming season. I felt that was a huge accomplishment for my rookie season.

And then all hell broke loose in southern Florida. That year, 2004, was the first time in history that Florida had been hit with four hurricanes (plus a tropical storm) in a single season. It seemed like as soon as we cleaned up after one hurricane, another one rolled in. I had just bought my first home – a double-wide on a half acre in La Belle, Florida. The hurricanes forced us to evacuate three different times, and we suffered serious roof and water damage – which in turn caused serious damage to paychecks and credit cards. We were without power for a long time and that meant there was no power to pump gas. We couldn't get back and forth to work but we still had to pay our bills, so I – just like a lot of people – had to turn to credit cards to keep things rolling. I worked with the insurance companies to try to get help, but it was a long and drawn out process and I ended up losing most of what I'd worked hard to accumulate. After all was said and done – mainly because the insurance company determined that the effects of a hurricane were excluded from coverage – I got a check for a measly $480. You read it right. Less than $500! As much as I didn't want government assistance, things were really bad and so I applied for help from FEMA. I was promptly turned down and left to fend for myself. As bad as my situation was, mine was just one story out of the millions of Floridians who lost their homes, incomes and spirit.

The people who ran the Bassmasters program stepped up right away. A lot of the pro fishermen were hit hard by these hurricanes, and so the tournament directors said that they would hold our slots for the following year if we weren't able to finish out the 2004 season. There was no way I'd be able to fish, so I was very appreciative of their support and understanding. I had qualified for the Elite 100 that's featured on ESPN; and I was comforted that, once I got through with getting my house and family back in order, I could go back to my fishing career without losing a beat. That sense of comfort, however, did not last very long. When I received my Bassmasters Tour package I learned that my entry fees were increasing from $14,000 to $55,000. That was a heartbreaker. I had boat sponsors and tackle sponsors, and even had a field sponsor to help me out a little bit; but it was just way out of my means to come up with $55,000 in entry fees. Unless you have a very wealthy family, a trust fund or a corporate sponsor, it's next to impossible to finance a Bassmasters career on your own. So the bottom line is that I had to give up my slot. Dreams do come true, but sometimes they also get broken.

I returned to fishing in FLW tournaments and earned a place in the EverStart Challenge Championships, but I started having more and more physical troubles. My back is completely mangled. Most people think pro fishing – or any professional sport – is a glamorous way of life. And it is great in so many ways. I love the challenge and I love the competition, but it puts a ton of stress on the human body. A lot of the guys on the tour have suffered major spinal damage and other serious injuries and chronic ailments. When you watch the highlight reels on ESPN, you see the beautiful scenery and serene lakes; and you see us catching one fish after another. What you don't see is how nasty and rough it can be. When you're competing in a tournament, you've got to fish. You're fishing for a living; you're fishing for money and for your family. So unless it's near-hurricane conditions, the tournament goes on. I've fished in snowstorms. I've fished in rain so heavy that when you walked out your hotel room in the morning it was like a waterfall coming off the roof and it didn't stop until you got back to the hotel that night. And it might be like that for days on end. Everything you owned would be drenched. If you were pleasure fishing, you'd have to be a total idiot to think about putting a boat in the water under those conditions. But as professionals, that's exactly what we were paid to do. The show must go on.

It's a tough life, but you know what? I can't wait to get back out there and start competing again. It's been hard over the last five or six years to pass up some opportunities to go on tour. I'm doing some serious back therapy right now and it's coming along pretty well, so I'm hopeful that 2013 will be the year I get back in the game. There's a painful emptiness inside me. I miss all the boys and good friends that I tour with. Tournament fishing is such a big part of my life that I almost feel like I'm playing hooky from work. So I want to get back out there but I have the additional problem of being perceived as "old" at the age of 46. It's getting harder and harder to find corporate sponsors. They tend to want the young guys, especially if they're photogenic. I understand that, but I believe nothing counts as much as experience.

And in terms of experience, I wouldn't trade any of my pro fishing experiences – not even the eight-foot swells, torrential rains, gale force winds, near-death experiences, and the disappointing middle-of-the-pack finishes – for anything else in the world. I've been blessed by the good Lord to have an opportunity to do what a little boy dreamed about so many years ago.

Chapter 24

Bent But Not Broken

Several times in this book, I've described incidents as being "one of the scariest things that ever happened to me." It's pretty much impossible to truly rank order how scared you were at any particular moment compared to another, but trust me on this one: this near-death experience definitely ranks in the top three scary moments of my life.

My brother and I literally grew up on and around water. We've seen a lot of crazy boat owners; some of our friends have gotten seriously hurt in boating accidents; and I personally flipped two boats when I was a kid. I've seen commercial boats sink, and I've seen luxury yachts smash into rocks, throw their boaters in the water, and sink to the bottom. Unless you're an outright idiot, all this firsthand experience with boating accidents will convince you to take boating seriously and focus on safety. And that's why Chris and I have always tried to be "defensive boaters." We handle our own boats as safely and courteously as possible, and keep our eyes open for folks who don't strive to do the same. Unfortunately, no matter how well you handle your own boat and how closely you observe those around you, bad things can still happen. Really bad things.

Shortly after I won my first tournament, Chris and I were in his boat watching an FLW tournament on Lake Okeechobee. It was a big tournament and we were riding around the lake watching the pros and seeing what we could learn from their techniques. Okeechobee has a lot of boat trails around the perimeter that wind through tall saw grass, and we decided to explore one particular boat trail that looked interesting. Now in the interests of full disclosure, we knew that these boat trails could be dangerous. Most of them have sharp curves and crossings, and they can be scary places when two or more boats are in the same general area. It's my hope that the conservation people will one day widen the trails to make them less dangerous.

Chris was driving the boat and he was right up against the saw grass. There was a curve up ahead of us and Chris was idling even slower than usual. And that probably saved our lives. If we'd been going faster, it would have been lights out forever. So we're practically at a standstill when a guy came around the curve in an 18-foot tunnel-hull boat. It was a lightweight aluminum boat, similar to a Jon boat but with a center console and a 90-hp motor. The guy saw us the same time we saw him. He steered the boat to his left to try to cut in on our starboard side but there wasn't enough room. Then he tried to cut back around to the right. Chris had our boat in full reverse trying to back up. In reality there was nothing either of could have done. There just wasn't enough time to react.

So he hit us not quite head-on, more like at about two o'clock. His boat caught on our trolling motor, forcing his bow to go up, which then clipped and caught on the pedestal seat of our boat. His boat flipped completely upside-down and went flying through the air. The last thing I remember is the sound of the outboard screaming when the boat came out of the water. I learned later that the boat had flipped over and landed on the passenger side of our boat – right where I had been sitting. The boat hit the dual console and sheared off both windshields. Just before the impact, I had instinctively ducked down by the console and that move saved me from being crushed. After the boat hit the console it fell to the floor of our boat and landed on my left arm. At the same time, something hit me in the head and knocked me unconscious. When the boat landed on my arm, it severed the muscles at the top of my forearm. The boat then rolled down my forearm onto my wrist, doing major tissue and cartilage damage, before rolling off into the water.

I came back to consciousness at the Buckhead Ridge locks and there was an ambulance waiting for me. The EMTs put my arm in something that looked like a long inner tube and then inflated it like a balloon. I could see that my arm was beaten up really bad, and I was thinking how I'd just had this arm operated on and how it was probably going to fall off if it had to deal with any more trauma. Well the good news is that, ever since I was a kid and had my wisdom teeth pulled out, doctors have told me that I had the strongest bones they've ever seen on a human. So I hadn't broken any bones but the cartilage, tendons, and muscles were torn up. And of course it had to be my left arm – the arm I do everything with. I know everyone favors one arm over the other, but I wasn't just left-handed – my right arm was pretty much useless. I think if I tried to pick my nose with my right hand I'd probably poke an eye out.

As soon as my head cleared I asked about Chris. I was terrified that he had been hurt worse than me. But he came out of it with some aches and pains and black-and-blues, and that was it. And the guy who crashed into us, made out the best of all. He'd been thrown about 30 yards away from the accident and landed safely in squishy swamp land.

The doctors patched up my arm and sent me home the same day. That night I couldn't sleep a wink. I just lay in bed hearing that outboard scream over the top of my head. At around three o'clock, I sat up in bed and saw Chris sitting in the doorway of my bedroom. He was still in a state of total shock and said he couldn't sleep either. I don't think either of us slept for several days. It was just a miracle that the flying boat didn't catch Chris or me and rip our heads off or slice us in half with its prop. It was a bone-chilling experience that still sends shivers up my spine when I think about it.

When I do think about that experience I also think about all the young people I see out on the water with high-performance bass boats, speed boats and jet skis. Way too many of these folks are going out on the water without basic common sense or any knowledge of the navigational laws that everybody's supposed to obey. If I were in charge of the world – and perhaps I should be – I would require everyone to take a safe-boating course and understand the basics. There's plenty of room on our waterways for everyone to use and enjoy. Having some knowledge and understanding of boating – along with the proper safety equipment – will only increase your enjoyment.

This accident that tore up my arm made my tournament fishing career all the more difficult. I had to suffer through a lot of painful physical therapy just to be able to tie on a hook or cast a line. My left arm is in pretty good shape now but it was a long, hard battle. I'm at a point where I feel like my body can't take much more trauma. I suffer with major back issues and I know part of it is due to that boat accident.

But through it all, I keep hunting and fishing. It

reminds me of some of the old guys that I worked construction with. These guys worked down in the ditches with a shovel all day long when they were in their late 50's and 60's. And I remember them saying that if they ever quit it would kill them. I heard the same thing from the old commercial fishermen I worked with. I guess the moral of the story is that when you're hard on your body, you have to keep your body moving. Because if you ever do stop moving, the shock to your system will be enough to kill you.

My work today is nowhere near as strenuous as when I was a commercial fisherman or construction worker, but tournament fishing and guiding are also demanding on your body and mind. In both cases there's a lot of standing. You might stand eight or ten hours at a time, and that makes for a very long and tiring day. If we do a full-day guided fishing trip of eight hours, the day starts an hour or more before we ever meet our customers to get all the equipment ready, drive to pick up the customers at their hotel, and then drive to the lake. And then at the end of the day, we have to clean up everything, put everything away, and check out the fishing reports to start planning for the next day. And to top it off, most of this happens out in the heat and sun of central Florida – an environment that is hard on the skin and physically draining. Tournament fishing involves all of these physical elements combined with the mental focus and toughness you need to compete at the highest level.

But I'm not complaining. I've always enjoyed hard work. I was taught from a very early age that if you wanted something, you had to work for it. I still take that to heart and still enjoy every moment on the water and in the woods. It's a magical experience that never loses its power over my heart and soul.

Chapter 25

Charity Begins At Home

I've never had much in my life, but whenever possible I've tried to give something back to help people and the community. Towards that end, I've been very fortunate to work as a fishing guide for an outfitting service that places a huge value on community service. Todd Kersey is the founder and owner of BassOnline.com. He's also my boss. I love and respect Todd for many reasons, but one of his most important qualities is his strong belief in making a positive difference in the local community and the world at large. Like all business owners, Todd runs the company to make a profit; but there's not an ounce of greed in him. What motivates him far more than money is the opportunity to make a lasting impact. Over the years Todd has gotten all of us involved in charitable events and programs; and it's been a great honor and privilege for me personally.

One of my strongest and most touching memories centers on our work with the Make-A-Wish Foundation. There was a 12-year-old young man who was suffering from a rare form of terminal cancer, and his last wish before he passed on was to accompany his family on a fishing trip to Lake Okeechobee. When we got the request, every single one of us wanted to help out and make it the best fishing experience anyone had ever had. We put our heads together and planned out a strategy on where to fish and what lures and bait to use.

When the young man arrived with his family, it was like having a celebrity around. We did everything we could to make him feel special. And that was easy to do because the boy was really friendly. You could see he was deathly ill, but he acted like any other kid – excited and happy to be doing something he loved with the people he loved most.

The first day on the water, he was catching a lot of good-sized bass. He was only able to fish for short stretches of time. In between, his mom or dad would give him an injection and he'd lie down and nap for a while. Then he'd get up and fish some more. The boy was unbelievably excited about the whole experience and having the time of his all-too-short life. The whole time, we were all cheering him on, but behind the sunglasses our eyes were welled with tears. It was a heart-wrenching scene but also a wonderful blessing to be part of. When the day ended, he'd caught some nice fish. He hadn't landed a super giant, but we were determined to get him one on the next trip.

The following day was focused on a trip to the local Bass Pro Shop. Now if you've never been to a Bass Pro Shop, you're missing out on a truly unique experience. This young man was blown away by the size of the store and the variety of equipment, and the Bass Pro Shop home office and local manager pretty much gave him the keys to the kingdom. He loaded up a cart with fishing equipment and it was all free. The generosity of everyone who met this young man reminded me of the way people come together during times of need. I think we're all genuinely good people at the core, but sometimes we get so caught up in the day-to-day nonsense of life that we don't take enough time to treasure the time we do have on earth.

The second day of fishing started out like the first. The young man caught a lot of medium-sized fish but no lunkers. He was having a blast, but we could see that he was more tired and had to rest more often than the first day. He was just about out of energy from the excitement and the effort of casting and reeling. We all knew we were getting close to having to call it a day, but we kept hoping and praying that he'd catch one of the big hawgs Okeechobee is famous for. Now I've never faltered in my belief in God, but when the boy's line went out straight and the rod tip bent over I looked up at the heavens and whispered a big thank-you. He had hooked a monster fish and it was pulling him from side to side in the boat. He was struggling with the rod but he wanted to land the fish himself and wouldn't accept help. So he's fighting the fish and laughing the whole time, and then the bass made a spectacular jump about ten yards from the boat. The boy's eyes were lit up with joy like I've never seen before or since. He finally landed the fish and got it in the boat. It was a certified Okeechobee monster and it was the icing on the cake and the finishing touch on an experience that none of us will ever forget.

It addition to Make-A-Wish, I've had the privilege of participating in the "Hot Rods & Reels" charity fishing tournament with some of the biggest names in NASCAR racing. All tournament proceeds benefit the Darrell Gwynn Foundation. Darrell Gwynn is a champion racer whose career ended in 1990 when he injured his spinal cord in a racing accident. I've gotten to know Darrell over the many years that I've participated in the tournament and I'm always impressed with how much he has accomplished in raising awareness of spinal cord injuries and teaching ways to prevent these life-changing injuries. The highlight of the event is seeing Darrell donate a custom-made power wheelchair to a deserving child or young adult. Just like with the Make-A-Wish program, it's one of those scenes where you're smiling and tearing-up at the same time.

When I first started fishing the Hot Rods & Reels tournaments, I really didn't know anything about NASCAR. I couldn't have named a driver if my life depended on it. The first driver I fished with was Geoff Bodine, who – I later learned – had won the Daytona 500 and many other major races. I had to ask his name a couple times because I'm not real good with remembering names. I can remember faces but not names, and Geoff got a kick out of the fact that I had no idea who he was and couldn't remember his name. Well neither of us will ever forget the other because Geoff and I won the very first Hot Rods & Reels tournament.

I always look forward to this tournament and over the years I've been able to fish with quite a few of the NASCAR drivers including Bill Elliott, Darrell Waltrip, and Jeff Burton. I've been paired up with Ryan Newman for the last five years. We haven't won a tournament together yet. In fact, we kind of stink but I enjoy fishing with him. We have a blast every time we get out on the water and Ryan is a super nice guy to hang out with. Lots of other NASCAR drivers, including big names like Tony Stewart, are involved with the Hot Rods & Reels program. It's a huge gathering of some really big-hearted folks and just good ole boys. It's fun for those of us who participate, and it's so important for the young people who benefit from the Foundation's generosity.

One of the most special activities I've ever been involved with – in conjunction with one of my fishing sponsors – is the Wounded Warriors Project. These events focus on the men and women – American soldiers –

returning from the wars in Iraq or Afghanistan with serious injuries. Their bodies are mangled and their minds are fixated on what's happened to them and the friends they left behind or lost forever. Anything you can do to get these folks to think about something else and add a little peace in their lives is a wonderful blessing. All of the young men and women I've met hold a special place in my heart and I still stay in touch with many of them to this day. I remember one soldier in particular who had lost his hand. Over the course of a couple of days, I taught him how to fish one-handed. He was a quick study and caught a bunch of fish during our time together; and he learned that it was something he'd be able to do and enjoy for the rest of his life. And that's the mindset that the Wounded Warriors Project tries to instill in these young people. Yes, your life will be different because of your injury; but your life isn't over and there will be plenty of opportunities to enjoy the world and the people around you.

I met another young man who was suffering from serious post-war depression. He lived up in the north country and felt particularly alone and isolated during the long, cold winters. He came down to Florida and I taught him how to fish; and he grabbed onto the sport as a way to keep active and focus on something positive. He's reached the point where he's interested in fishing some tournaments as a co-angler, and he now has a lifetime interest that will help keep his mind and body occupied

What I find most interesting about these charitable activities is that I – like most everyone who gets involved – do it to help others; but at the end of the day, I get just as much out of the program as the recipients of the charity's generosity. It helps me to take a step back and appreciate everything I have. And it helps me realize that life is short and that we should make every moment count. Every single moment.

Chapter 26

Man's Best Friend

By this point, you know that I love animals – big ones and small ones, furry ones and slimy ones, harmless ones and ferociously dangerous ones. But there is one animal that owns my heart. As I write this, my two precious miniature dachshunds, Penny and Cleo, are curled up on my lap; and all three of us are content with the world.

Dogs are truly magical creatures. They have a heart and spirit about them that perfectly complements the human soul and creates a lifelong bond.

My first dog growing up as a boy in Ohio was a full-blooded collie named Daisy. I used to love watching the old, black and white television series about a collie named Lassie. Our Daisy looked just like Lassie, the canine movie star, and was every bit as smart and loyal. One of my earliest memories of Daisy, and the special relationship between dogs and people, occurred at a family get-together on my grandparents' farm. We were having a hog roast and all the kids were out playing in the yard. One of my cousins did something that his mom thought was out of line and she went to spank him.

When she raised her hand, Daisy ran over to her, grabbed her by the wrist and pulled her away from the child. Daisy then released my aunt's wrist, but she stood there watching her and making sure that she didn't try to hit the child again. It was my first – and lasting – realization that animals are often more humane than humans.

All the dogs in my life have been viewed as and treated like family members. Dogs have been bred in all different shapes and sizes and intended for a variety of purposes. In every case, however, they've been breed to be man's best friend, and I'm proud and pleased to honor that relationship. I see it as a two-way street – no different than the relationship we have with any human friend. We provide for our dogs in the way of a home, food, exercise and love; and they repay us with unequivocal love. There is nothing like doggie love. Whenever I come home – whether from a trip to the grocery store or a weeklong fishing trip – Cleo and Penny are always the first ones to greet me at the door. Their tails are wagging with wild abandon, they're jumping up on their hind legs, and their eyes are fixated on my every move. They make me smile even if I've had a tough day at the office (figuratively, of course, because my office is a bass boat with a view that's a thousand times better than any Wall Street corner office). The shared love between dogs and humans can also cause pain and sadness – that's why the *Marley and Me* book and movie were so successful.

Daisy got sick when I was about four years old. My mom brought her to the veterinarian and came back home alone. She told us that Daisy had passed away and was up in heaven with her own mom and dad. I can still remember feeling sick to my stomach and being weighed down with an emptiness as I walked around the house and the yard where Daisy played. Everyone was crying and we hugged each other for consolation. That night at the dinner table I came to the realization that death was a natural part of life and all the animal protein that we shared was a key part of our relationship with the animal kingdom. We always said grace at dinner, but we never stopped at simply thanking God for the food on the table. We also took a moment at our dinner table to acknowledge all the beautiful animals we shared the earth with.

Not long after Daisy died, we got another collie and we named her Daisy as well. Daisy got in the family way with a local German shepherd and we kept one of the pups, Dusty, who quickly became my best friend in all the world. Despite being a mixed breed, Dusty looked pretty much like a full-blooded collie. Dusty and Daisy accompanied Chris and me as we played in the woods and visited the local farms to fish in all the different ponds. Those two dogs, mother and daughter, stayed right beside us and kept close watch over us everywhere we went. When we moved to Florida, Dusty and Daisy came with us, but they had a pretty hard time adjusting because the Florida heat is difficult for long-haired breeds. Daisy died of old age but Dusty got hit by a car. I remember holding her in my arms in the back of the truck as my mother drove her to the vet. I knew in my heart that these would be the last moments I'd ever spend with her, and my fears were confirmed when the vet said there was nothing he could do to save her. We said our goodbyes and then the vet put her down. I sobbed on the way home and wondered if life would always be full of these horrible deaths and sorrowful partings.

It would be.

Shortly after Dusty died, my mom got us an eight-week-old Doberman puppy. She was a sweet, absolutely beautiful Dobie who loved everyone. She quickly became a fixture around the hotel, but she never lost her energetic puppy ways. When she was still a young dog, she pushed her way out the front door and went running through the yard. She ended up in the road and got hit by a car. I wasn't home to see it, but I re-experienced that gut-wrenching hurt when my mom told me what had happened and that we had lost another beloved member of our family. We got a second Doberman and I'm happy to say that she lived to grow old and gray. That doesn't happen nearly often enough. The saddest thing about dogs is they do have short lives. The lifespan of a big dog typically ranges from 8 to 12 years old, with smaller dogs averaging 12 to 16 years. Any way you count it, it's an extremely short life – especially when you consider that you'd be happy to spend the rest of your life with each and every one of them. So the point with dogs, as it is with all of our loved ones, is to make every moment count.

The first dog that I personally owned was an English pointer named Cy. She was a bird dog and she lived to hunt. Cy was a wonderful companion and one of the smartest dogs I've ever been around. Cy got very sick when she was only five years old. My brother and I drove on ice-covered roads all over Ohio to different veterinarians and animal hospitals. I spent every bit of money I had saved – literally thousands of dollars – trying to save Cy's life, but it wasn't to be. I grieved for days and had to ask Chris to bury her in the frozen ground because I was too broken up to do it myself.

My heart was broken over Cy's death, and my friends and family did everything possible to try and console me. One of my good friends in Ohio was Cecil Strong, who did a lot of bird dog work in the state. Cecil got me involved in doing field trials and working with dogs, and after I lost Cy he asked me to come over to his house. When I got there he led me out back to his kennel. As soon as I stepped into the kennel a gang of little white things started crawling over my feet and climbing up my legs. They were English setter bird dogs. And not just any litter of English setters, some of the best bred English setters I'd ever seen. Cecil gave me a puppy that I named Angel, and Angel is still alive today. She's old, but she's had a wonderful life and has given my family and me so much joy and so many precious memories.

Cy and Angel were both hunting dogs. I'm not much of a bird hunter, but I enjoy doing a little bit of it here and there. When I've been out in the field I've always loved watching bird dogs at work. They are so incredibly alive and alert when doing what they were bred to do. I recently had an opportunity to visit Kansas and take part in a pheasant hunt. We were hunting with three black Labrador retrievers. Now I've always been around Labs as pets, and they are certainly one of the finest family dogs you can imagine. But watching these dogs respond to their handler's commands and hand signals was truly a sight to behold. They were just so excited to be out in the open and pleasing their master. And when we did shoot down a bird, they ran to fetch it and bring it back to you; and all they wanted in return was a pat on the head and affirmation that they did a good job. These dogs were Labs, but I've seen the same thing with beagles chasing rabbits, bird dogs working for ducks, and hounds chasing down a wild hog. These are animals that love working with people to accomplish a common goal.

I sometimes wish that people were as pure and good-hearted as dogs. I do believe that most people are good by nature, but there are way too many mean people in the world. And the worst SOBs in my book are those people who are mean to animals. In my book (and this is my book, after all), if a person can't treat a dog or other animal with basic decency, they probably can't treat humans decently either; and they just suck through and through. I'm sure that sounds harsh, but I've seen people be mean to dogs a couple times in my life, and it just makes me want to beat the snot balls out of their freakin' heads. It's truly pathetic that somebody could be cruel to a sweet and defenseless animal. I know there are idiots out there that purposely swerve their car to try and hit a dog, squirrel, possum or whatever animal is crossing the road. Some people get a kick out of that stuff, but it makes me want to puke.

I guess the reason this topic is so emotional for me is that I have personal experience with some people's total disregard for the value of a dog's life. When I was in Ohio and Angel was still a young dog, I adopted a chow puppy from a moron who just wanted to take it out back and put a bullet through its head. The poor thing was being abused and, as you would imagine, he didn't like anyone – including me. He was just a little fireball, a little ball of red fuzz, and I named him Ninja. At first he wouldn't come to me, but instead kept circling around keeping a curious and nervous eye on me. I kept him with me everywhere I went and over time he came to trust me and became a loyal and loving pet. Because I had Angel as my daily companion, I gave Ninja to my brother and they became inseparable. It was a perfect arrangement because Chris and I were best friends, and Angel and Ninja had become best friends as well. Chows are very protective, and Ninja watched over our family and treated newcomers with suspicion until one of us gave a sign that the person could be trusted. Ninja grew old with us but then came down with cancer and died in my brother's lap with my hand patting his shoulder. We buried Ninja in my backyard; and as sad as we were to lose him, we were happy for the time we had shared and that we had saved him from a cruel and early death.

Every one of my dogs has had a magical effect on me,

and I hope that God has reserved a special place in heaven where we get to be reunited with our pets. Actually, that's not just my hope – it's my belief.

Chapter 27

A Guiding Life

Looking back, I feel confident in saying that I've been a fishing guide ever since I was ten years old when I first moved to Florida. Between my mom and my grandmother I learned that the most important part of our job was making sure the guests of our fishing resort went home with happy and long-lasting memories. I loved teaching our guests how to rig a line, how to cast, and when to set the hook. When I got a little older, I'd take guests out on boats and teach them where the different species of fish hung out and the different types of bait to use depending on the time and situation. It was the same way with my friends. Despite growing up on the island, a lot of my neighborhood friends didn't know much about fishing and were more interested in team sports and meeting girls; and I was always excited when I converted one of them and showed them the excitement and challenge of fishing. So I guess the idea of life as a fishing guide was always in the back of my mind.

That idea came to the front burner during my recuperation from the arm and hand surgery I had during the end of my stay in Ohio. I was in a cast and wasn't able to fish myself but I sure enjoyed taking all my different friends fishing. Every chance I got, I'd take somebody out on the boat and just spend a day with them on the water. It was something fun to do that got me out of the house and allowed me to breathe some nice fresh air away from traffic and noise.

Once I got to Florida I studied to get my captain's license and learned how to be a bass fishing guide. My whole life I've been blessed to have people in my life who went out of their way to help me, and that's exactly how I got started as a guide. One of the guys I fished with in the Gator division was Todd Kersey. Todd was a super guy, a good fisherman, and a straight shooter. I always enjoyed hanging out and chatting with him; and when he founded his company, BassOnline.com, I ended up going to work for him as a guide. The company started out small with just a few of us, but it's grown into the largest outfitter in South Florida. We have guides that work on Lake Kissimmee, Toho, the Everglades and all over central Florida. My focus – which should come as no surprise – is Lake Okeechobee.

A lot of time I feel that my life has come full circle. I used to love to fish as a young boy on Okeechobee, and now I have the opportunity to introduce this beautiful lake and the sport of bass fishing to a whole new generation of young people. I've taken a lot of families out fishing on Okeechobee and, at the end of the trip, the kids have told me that it was more fun than Disney World. That's high praise and makes me grin from ear to ear every time I recall those words and remember how a child's eyes lit up when he or she was reeling in their first fish. It's truly magical – and I would have to agree that it's even more magical than the Magic Kingdom.

There's only one Lake Okeechobee. It's arguably America's best fishery – and perhaps the best fishery in the world. That's why we host visitors from all over the world and why we have clients who come back every single year. That's one of the things I love about guiding. I get to meet a wide range of people from all walks of life, all ages and nationalities, and all skill levels. When we're out on the water it doesn't matter if you're a doctor or doorman, a professor or plumber, a barber or biochemist. We're all out there to catch some fish, enjoy the spectacular beauty of the lake, and marvel at the gators, herons, osprey and other wildlife that roam the waters, shores, and open air of Okeechobee. My goal for every trip is to give my clients an adventure and memory that they can take home with them and treasure. And if I can share some new techniques and "trade secrets" that can help lift their skill level to new heights, that's even better because they'll remember their trip to Okeechobee every time they cast into their local waters and reel in a keeper or a schoolie.

The really cool thing about guiding is that my clients aren't the only ones who make memories to last a lifetime. I get to share in those memories. One hot summer day I was out with a young husband and wife from New York. We were catching some pretty good-sized fish, and the wife hooked onto one that looked to be about three pounds. Well the fish jumped up in the air and threw the bait. The wife hardly had time to be disappointed because as soon as the bait hit the water a six-and-a-half-pounder grabbed it, so she effectively doubled the size of her fish. I've been fishing my whole life so I had seen that happen before. But I'd never seen it happen twice in the same day. But that's exactly what happened. The husband got a three-pounder on the line. It jumped up, threw the bait, and when the bait landed back in the water it was hit by a six-pounder. Like I always say, every day on Okeechobee brings a unique adventure.

My most unique guiding experience happened a few years ago, but to really provide a sense of just how crazy it was

I have to go back twenty years. I was fishing up on Blue Cypress Lake with my childhood buddy, Walt. Blue Cypress was absolutely beautiful. Like its name suggests, there were Cypress trees everywhere. The lake offered every conceivable type of fish habitat. There were stumps and grass beds, deep open water and shallow marshy areas. It had the look of a place where you'd get a bite on every cast, but looks can be awfully deceiving. We fished there all day and never got so much as a nibble. So the day was winding down and I was idling through some stumps, and Walt suggested we call it a day. "There's no fish in this pond," he said. Well, on the souls of everyone I've ever known and loved, as soon as he said there weren't any fish in the pond, a five-pounder jumped out of the water and landed right between us. It was flipping and flopping all over the deck and Walt and I watched it in total shock. Then we started laughing so hard we could hardly breathe. We put the fish back in the water and headed home, realizing there was nothing else we could do to top that.

So fast-forward twenty years. I was fishing in the Everglades with one of my longtime clients, Allen. Allen was an ex-Marine, a true gentleman and a ball to fish with. He came down just about every year to fish five or six days at a time. This particular time we were fishing down in the Everglades and we were having a really good day catching nice-sized bass on top with poppers and the like. Allen turned to me and asked, "Mark, have you ever had one of these big old bastards jump in the boat?" I started to laugh and was about to tell him the story about Walt and me when a fish about four pounds jumped right in the boat. We were up against a saw grass edge, and the fish must have been chasing something it wanted and jumped just a bit too high. Well Allen just about had a shit fit. He went nuts, laughing and carrying on, just not believing what had happened. And I was kind of in shock that such a strange thing had happened to me twice in my life. I guess it proves one of two things – either bass or God has a good sense of humor.

While I'm not a Floridian by birth, I am a Floridian through and through. I love the state and I take a lot of pride in our tourism industry. And I take my responsibility seriously. People save and plan all year for their vacations, and I want to make every moment count – from the time when I pick them up at their hotel to the time I drop them off. Todd once told me about a vacation he'd taken with his family where a lot of things got messed up and the people he dealt with didn't seem to care and didn't make an effort to improve the situation. It left a sour taste in his mouth and he vowed that his company, and the people he hired, would always make the customer's experience our top priority. Sometimes Mother Nature throws a wrench into the game, and things get a little tough; but no matter what, we always go down swinging and put our heart and soul into every trip.

While I still have hopes that my back will heal enough to let me compete again, guiding will always be my primary life and vocation. So many people have jobs that they hate or simply put up with because they need the paycheck. I have a job that I truly love, that I'm good at, and that makes people happy. I couldn't ask for more and I thank the good Lord every day for blessing me with a job that gives me the opportunity to meet people from all around the world and help create joyful memories that will never fade.

Epilogue

Giving Thanks

We only go around once in this world. Our time on Earth is limited and precious. We have a responsibility to serve as conscientious stewards for all that Earth, nature and the heavens provide us. And we're not just stewards for future generations, we're also stewards for past generations. That, in my opinion, is where we fall short.

One of the first lessons I learned in life was to "listen to your elders." And I wasn't unique in that regard. Most kids heard that refrain repeated over and over by their parents. The reason is simple: wisdom follows from experience and old folks have a lot more experience than young people. Unfortunately this passing along of knowledge and experience from one generation to the next doesn't happen very much any more. You can blame it on technology, changing morals, a more hectic pace of life, or whatever; but the fact remains that many Americans would not be able to survive if they were forced to live like their grandparents or great-grandparents. As a society, we're losing a grip on our past and have lost many of our basic life skills. How many people today know how to start a fire, can vegetables, make preserves, or cure meat to store it safely without refrigeration? How many people would even know how to plant a garden and rotate the crops through the four seasons? It's a small fraction of the population. It's just so much easier and more convenient – and a lot less work – to go to the supermarket and buy something that's virtually tasteless, packed with all kinds of chemical preservatives and maybe even processed as far away as China. We bring the stuff home from the store, put it on a shelf and don't think about or care about where it came from.

Some of my fondest (non-fishing) memories as a child back in Ohio were planting seeds and watering the garden, sitting on the porch with my family snapping green beans, and watching my mom and grandmother can fruits and vegetables to get us through the winter. Yes it was hard work, but it was also fun and it was something that we did together as a family.

This is an issue I talk about a lot because I worry about what would happen if our nation ever suffered a serious military attack or natural disaster. For example, most people don't realize how fragile our national power grid is. I know it's got a bunch of fail-safes built into it; but if we lost electrical power in large parts of the country, there would be panic in the streets because the majority of people wouldn't know what to do. We've seen this on a smaller scale with Hurricanes Katrina and Charley. People join hands and work together at first, but it doesn't last long. Once all the food is gone from the supermarkets and the looters start coming out, it becomes a very scary place. In only a matter of days, people would be forced to live much like their ancestors did over a hundred years ago. They'd be no heat. Emergency broadcast systems would be of no value because our televisions, radios, and phones wouldn't work. Gas stations might have gasoline in the tanks, but the pumps wouldn't work. Food would spoil and hungry stomachs will make people do some seriously bad things. Just think about what you would do if your children were hungry. Is there anything you wouldn't do to get them food?

I think this all goes to show how separated we have become from nature. Part of it is due to the rise of huge cities and their sprawling suburbs. Many people live hundreds or thousands of miles away from their food source, and they never get to see animals in the wild (other than squirrels and pigeons). From my perspective, this separation from animals has had a major negative impact on our lives. Except for our pet dogs and cats, most people have never had a relationship with an animal, either domesticated or wild. If you go back in time, animals were precious to people – even the animals that were hunted or raised for slaughter. I'm a self-educated person. I never spent much time in a classroom. Everything I've learned has been a hands-on education. I've worked on ranches and farms at various times in my life. I've worked with hogs, cattle, and chickens, and I've seen how well these farmers treated their animals. They fed them well, exercised and nurtured them to grow up strong and healthy. And, sure, you can argue that it was in their own self-interest because a healthy animal is worth more than an unhealthy one; but the overriding reason was a sense of concern, fairness, and deep affection for their animals. I believe that American farmers and ranchers set a high standard for the rest of the world in terms of an ethical approach to animal management. Being the rugged individualists that America is known for, our ranchers and farmers also understand that there is always room for improvement and they strive to keep getting better.

I would say the same thing about American hunters. It's a very sad commentary on our society that hunting has increasingly been viewed as something evil that is only done by dumb rednecks or beer-bellied bullies. Let me state this clearly and concisely: Hunting is not a *necessary evil*. It's a *necessary part* of life if we want to continue to co-exist with animals. Hunting is a heritage that's been around ever since America was founded and for tens of thousands of years beforehand. It's not animal cruelty; it's the natural order of things and helps maintain the delicate balance between nature and humans' ever-increasing desire to build and expand. I've noticed that the people who are most opposed to hunting are the ones who are the least educated about the ways of our native wildlife. I would urge everyone who picks up this book to share it with someone who tends to pass judgment on hunting and hunters.

And I would also remind the anti-hunting masses of one important fact. When hunters and their families gather around the dinner table to share the bounty of freshly harvested venison, wild boar or turkey, they give a sincere thank-you to the Lord for their bounty. They don't give lip service; they give a very thoughtful and heartfelt thank-you. Hunters understand that God created animals to help keep man healthy and strong; and they understand they have a responsibility to choose their prey carefully, become proficient with their weapons, and maximize the utilization of every harvested animal.

None of this is meant to suggest that we should turn back the clock. I'm not against progress. I just want to help ensure that we don't throw out all the good old stuff in favor of new stuff that, in the end, may not actually work out so well.

Like many Americans, I'm concerned about the issues we face and the direction we're heading. We have to fix a lot of problems and overcome a lot of obstacles, but we've had to do that before and always succeeded. Things are certainly crazy right now. The far right is too extreme, and the far left is too extreme. The reality is – and always has been – in the middle. No one is all right and no one is all wrong. We just need to go back to our Founding Fathers' vision and treat each individual with respect and compassion. It sounds so simple when you say it; and it is pretty simple.

America is jam-packed with honest and hard-working people, and those are the people that have made America great. It hasn't been the President or the Congress or the Supreme Court that have made us the greatest and most successful country the world has ever known. It's been the spirit and dedication of Americans who have gotten their hands dirty building roads, bridges, homes and schools. It's been the entrepreneurial Americans who were inspired to start their own businesses, invent new products, and build a better life for themselves, their family, their community, and their country. America was built by people with drive and ambition. True Americans have never been content to rest on their laurels or expect a handout or free ride. We take pride in what we have because we worked hard to get it.

I'm one of those people. And though I don't have a lot to show for it; I've led a life that 99% of the people in the world can only dream about.

I'm thankful that I've made it this far, and I'll take every additional day the Lord throws my way as something to be treasured.

Acknowledgments

I owe a great debt of gratitude to so many people who have blessed me with their friendship.

Two folks who deserve extra special thanks are my good friends, John and Jennifer Oatley. John has been like a father to me, and both he and Jennifer provided much needed financial support after the hurricanes of 2004.

I also want to thank all my friends and colleagues at BassOnLine.com – especially my boss and good friend, Todd Kersey. The Okeechobee and South Florida community has also been very helpful including all the people at Slim's Fish Camp, Jolly Roger Marina, Chuck Anderson and Brothers, Robert Ashley, John Beondo, Rodney, David & Jack Black, Craig Bennett, Warren Burkhardt, Chris Christopher, Danny Clontz, Walt & Mike Donaldson, Bob Feltner, Jeff Freeland, Sam Gerhard, Tom Hale, Ron & Jennifer Harless, Pop Hasselgrove & Family, Karen Hughes-Hart, Jetty Bait & Tackle (Don), LP & Luke Johnson, Paul Kaptis, Cicle Lane, Mike Lame, Danny Miller, Brant McManus, Mike McHale, Tom Meredith & Family, Fr. Richard Pobjecky & Family, Bill Penn, Kristie & Karrie Regester, Jim Ryan, Ben Race, Don E. Root, Alfred & Jerry Sanderlin, St. Andrews Church, Tom Schliesman, Wayne Stitzel, Jack & Betty Sullivan, Steve Shepard, Tim, David & Sam Summerlin, Donald Stiller, Mark Welsh, Ken Whittaker, Steve Wilson, Willie & Slick, and John Work.

Special acknowledgement is also due to my

tournament co-anglers and traveling buddies Jim Anderson, Jim Barnick, Galen Fugh, and Larry Martgolio.

Nothing in my life, however, would have come to pass without the love and support of my family: Gary Shepard, Mayme & Mart Shepard, Sherry Shepard, Shawn Clapper, Missie Finan, Clyde & Mary Jane Becker, and Melissa & Marky Shepard.

And last but certainly not least, I want to thank you, Mom, for teaching me that hard work and honesty are the character traits that make the man. Thank you, Dad, for lifelong lessons on using firearms safely and wisely. Thank you, Chris, for sharing a lifetime of laughter, tears and adventure. Thank you, Kadie and Jess, for being the loving daughters you are. And thank you to my wife, K.C., for sharing my home and my heart.

16732070R00127